ON RETIRING WELL

A GUIDEBOOK FOR RETIREMENT PLANNING OVER 50

This book contains general information that may not be suitable for everyone. The information contained herein should not be construed as personalized investment advice. There is no guarantee that the views and opinions expressed in this book will come to pass. Investing in the stock market involves gains and losses and may not be suitable for all investors. Information presented herein is subject to change without notice and should not be considered as a solicitation to buy or sell any security. Hunt Country Wealth Management, Chris Merchant does not offer legal or tax advice. Please consult the appropriate professional regarding your individual circumstance. ***Past performance is no guarantee of future results.***

Printing in the United States of America
First Printing 2024

ISBN: 978-1-7339648-1-4 Paperback
ISBN: 978-1-7339648-2-1 Ebook
ISBN: 978-1-7339648-3-8 Hardcover

Cover designed by Najdan Mancic, Iskon Design

For inquiries, please reach out to the author through the following channels:

Website: huntcountryinvestments.com

Email: advisor@huntcountryinvestments.com

TABLE OF CONTENTS

To Heather Merchant, my partner in both business and life. This book is dedicated to you in gratitude for the light you bring into every venture we undertake.

AUTHOR'S FORWARD

Although you just opened a book about the importance of retirement planning, I must tell you that your transition to retirement and life thereafter won't always go exactly as planned. However, the act of planning itself is invaluable in helping you navigate whatever challenges may come your way. One of my favorite quotes, attributed to Dwight D. Eisenhower, the Supreme Allied Commander in WW2 and subsequently the 34th President of the United States, comes to mind: "Plans are nothing; planning is everything." While our actual outcomes often differ from our plans, the process of planning equips us with the knowledge, foresight, and adaptability needed to navigate life's uncertainties, including those during the final years leading up to retirement and beyond.

Retirement, akin to life, is susceptible to unforeseen twists and turns. Despite meticulous planning, unexpected variables can upend even the most meticulously designed retirement plans. Life's surprises, such as health challenges or shifts in the financial situations of our loved ones, possess the ability to significantly reshape our retirement strategies. This underscores the significance of adaptability in planning for retirement.

My aim in writing this book is to create a comprehensive model, a kind of checklist, to guide you in ensuring that your transition to retirement and life thereafter is well thought through. This preparation will grant you the liberty to adapt to life's demands. By considering all the factors outlined, you will be better equipped to handle those expected challenges that may come your way. While unexpected events may arise, your proactive planning will empower you to navigate through them more effectively.

I've had the honor of collaborating with incredibly bright-minded clients. They showcase exceptional analytical abilities, meticulously crafting spreadsheets to outline their financial paths. These tools are vital for their preparation, and I'm happy to assist in creating similar resources. However, it's important to recognize that these serve as guidelines, not rigid templates. The essence of financial planning for retirement is found in living a rich and satisfying life marked by diminished financial concerns and improved financial choices rather than obsessively tracking every cent for the rest of your days.

After completing this book, you will not only have a clear vision of what an effective roadmap for your financial future entails but will also give you the confidence to adjust it as circumstances change. Welcome to your journey toward a well-planned retirement.

GUIDANCE ON USING THIS BOOK

This book is organized to effectively help you grasp its concepts. Following the logical sequence helps ensure a smooth flow of ideas, enriching your learning journey. Moreover, you can utilize it as a guide by referring to the table of contents for topics of interest. My primary aim is to deliver valuable information in a manner that resonates with you. While certain chapters may not be relevant to your needs, others could be precisely what you're seeking, so please feel free to jump around as you see fit.

Despite not being a professional writer, I have endeavored to maintain clarity and conciseness. I acknowledge that this book may not be a riveting read, but I aspire for it to offer value in its own authentic way. Perhaps not in terms of entertainment but in genuine substance. I have devoted numerous hours to writing and my entire career to acquiring the insights and knowledge you will discover within these pages. I genuinely hope you find it beneficial.

I have no illusions of creating a bestseller for the masses. My aim is for this book to benefit my current clients and potentially aid future ones in their transition to retirement and beyond. If they, and by chance someone beyond my usual readers who find this book, glean something valuable from it and improves their financial well-being and quality of life as a result then I will have achieved my goal.

BOOK INTRODUCTION

This book delves into the art of preparing for your transition to retirement and life afterward. Despite the abundance of resources on financial planning and retirement, many lack practicality on managing finances in this stage of your life. Prioritizing practical advice, my aim is to craft a functional guide to support your successful retirement journey.

Contemplating retirement can be overwhelming. Even individuals I've assisted in their retirement planning have initially felt uncertain. Excited yet somewhat lost, they are unsure of the right questions to ask. These are intelligent individuals who have achieved success, saved diligently, and made sound decisions. However, their focus has been on running businesses, raising families, and embracing life, leaving little time for retirement planning. Therefore, this book aims to provide people like these with the framework and guidance needed to retire well.

Let me clarify why I consider this book essential for you:

1. Retirement marks a significant life transition demanding careful consideration. With the right mindset and knowledge, the changeover to retirement and life beyond can become a truly remarkable phase of your life. It is my aspiration that this book guides you toward a fulfilling retirement.

2. Misinformation about finances and retirement is widespread. Depending on unreliable sources may lead to regrettable consequences. I aim to furnish you with genuine, precise, and impartial information.

3. A thoughtfully planned retirement will often surpass expectations. I believe that "well-planned" doesn't necessarily equate to being difficult to plan. By adopting the right mindset, utilizing proper resources, and perhaps seeking a bit of assistance, you can do this.

Retirement is a unique phase of life that requires a fresh approach to managing finances. Recognizing the need for adjustments is the initial step toward planning for a successful retirement. But before investing any more of your time reading this book, let's ensure it meets your needs.

IS THIS THE RIGHT BOOK FOR YOU?

This book is tailored for individuals aged 50 or older who plan to retire within the next five years. They have diligently saved and built a nest egg, with personal savings being their primary source of retirement income. Searching for a reliable retirement plan that allows for flexibility to adjust to evolving needs, they emphasize stability and security for their retirement years. The concepts and strategies in this book resonate most with individuals who prioritize retirement stability and security over metrics such as ROI "Return on Investment" or aggressive investment tactics.

Most of these individuals have worked in the private sector, which has provided a steady income enabling them to accumulate savings over the years. This means that they might not have had equivalent retirement saving chances as self-employed persons or government workers with benefits like pensions or substantial business equity. Creating a retirement plan that helps ensure stability and security presents a unique challenge for this group.

Exceptions exist. Individuals who own successful businesses they plan to sell as they near retirement may benefit from this book. Selling a business can result in a substantial cash inflow, necessitating careful planning for a sustainable retirement. The book provides guidance on managing and investing these assets effectively to create a steady income stream.

Another exception is when one spouse is a government employee with a TSP plan and a pension and the other has personal savings from working in the private sector. In such cases, couples navigating these scenarios can find value in this book as they seek a strategic financial path for their family.

The strategies discussed in this book are most beneficial for individuals with savings exceeding $500,000. If your nest egg falls below this threshold, alternative strategies focusing on leveraging social security benefits and identifying supplementary income sources may be more suitable.

For those who meet these criteria and have a thirst for knowledge, this book can be a valuable resource. Over the course of your career, you have likely witnessed significant changes in retirement trends, observing shifts in how people approach retirement. Let's begin by exploring this evolution together to equip you for the road ahead.

PART I

SETTING THE STAGE FOR YOUR RETIREMENT

CHAPTER 1

THE CHANGING LANDSCAPE OF RETIREMENT

In the past thirty or so years as you dedicated yourself to your career, retirement has significantly transformed. The days of retiring with a pension and a gold watch are now uncommon, especially in the private sector. Pensions are becoming less reliable as a post-career income source. Unlike before, where pensions offered a fixed income based on service years and final salary, today's trend is moving toward plans like 401(k)s and IRAs. This change shifts the financial burden from employers to employees, emphasizing the need for proactive retirement planning.

While this shift presents challenges, it also offers increased flexibility. Nowadays, individuals have the freedom to choose their retirement timing and manage their investments, granting them more control over their retirement journey. However, this autonomy requires strong financial acumen and understanding of investment principles. Establishing a reliable financial framework post-retirement is essential for a steady income stream, akin to a pension plan.

Amidst these transformative times as you approach retirement and consider your next steps, a favorite quote comes to mind: "Reaching the summit is only half the journey." Let's explore the mental and financial shifts required to realize the freedom and flexibility offered by this modern retirement era.

CHAPTER 2

THE MOUNTAIN CLIMBING ANALOGY

While adventurers fantasize about conquering the summit of Mount Everest and reveling in the achievement, they often underestimate the grueling descent. Similarly, retirement planning usually emphasizes the accumulation phase, focusing on working and saving, while neglecting the distribution stage. Exploring the Everest analogy offers deeper insights into this journey.

Most climbers nearing Everest's final ascent are in peak physical condition. They catch sight of the summit, envisioning the triumphant moment of reaching the peak. This anticipation is well-deserved. The journey thus far demanded not only physical strength but also unwavering dedication and commitment—scaling this height is a remarkable feat.

Nevertheless, as climbers near the summit, they enter the most perilous part of their expedition: the infamous *Death Zone*. Situated above 8000 meters, this stretch includes the final push to the summit and the initial descent. Oxygen scarcity, extreme temperatures, and treacherous terrain render this zone lethal, with most fatalities occurring here. Even minor missteps can lead to grave consequences. Harsh weather conditions or injuries in this zone significantly decrease survival chances. However, once climbers successfully navigate the death zone, the subsequent journey becomes comparatively less hazardous.

Similarly, many soon-to-be retirees approach retirement's threshold in sound financial health. They are likely earning more money than at any other point in their career and they have substantial retirement savings. Standing on the brink of retirement, they anticipate the exhilaration of this milestone. They may already be picturing retirement parties or planning long-awaited vacations. However, this juncture also brings financial risks akin to the onset of Everest's *Death Zone*. Retirement has its own *Danger Zone*.

During the pivotal retirement phase known as the *Danger Zone*, you'll navigate the period leading up to retirement and the early post-retirement years. This term highlights the fragility of this time, marked by numerous financial challenges. Although errors during this period may not be immediately catastrophic, given retirement's longevity, even minor misjudgments can escalate into significant issues affecting later years when financial management capabilities diminish. Furthermore, unforeseen economic downturns such as a stock market crash or severe recession could potentially arise during this vulnerable period. Nevertheless, successful navigation through this tumultuous phase is likely to pave the way for a more stable retirement journey ahead.

Recognizing the vulnerability surrounding your early retirement years is critical. This period demands meticulous attention and strategic planning. Throughout this guide, I will furnish strategies and tools to navigate this challenging phase with confidence.

Comprehending retirement transcends mere acknowledgement of its arrival. It signifies the initiation of a new life chapter, necessitating a distinct approach to financial strategies. Transitioning from the accumulation phase to the distribution phase and navigating the *Danger Zone* while managing resources to help ensure sustained income throughout retirement is pivotal. I will delve deeper into this concept for clarity.

CHAPTER 3

THE RETIREMENT ZONES™

To delve deeper into the nuances between the Accumulation and Distribution phases and provide a structured approach for people to adapt and employ strategies specific to their retirement journey, I've devised a model called *The Retirement Zones™*. This model allows individuals to identify their location in the retirement journey and implement targeted strategies. The experience of each retiree may indeed differ, but the general trajectory and challenges encountered are often quite similar. Within the model I've crafted, five distinct retirement zones exist, each with its own characteristics and challenges.

RETIREMENT ZONE 1: THE ASCENT—WORKING AND SAVING (ACCUMULATION)

If you're reading this book, you're likely very familiar with *Zone 1:, Working Years*, as you've spent the last 30+ years there. I assume you've excelled and been successful in this phase. Even though you're nearly done with this zone, it's crucial to revisit this segment to comprehend the factors that have led to success here and how they may require adjustments in the upcoming zones. Fully grasping this is key to your journey ahead.

Zone 1 marks the beginning of your professional journey, akin to starting at the base of a mountain. The initial years are challenging as you navigate through career hurdles and the delicate balancing act of managing expenses while saving. As you progress up the slope gaining career traction, the path ahead becomes clearer. You begin to adjust to the increasing financial responsibilities and investments essential for future aspirations, especially retirement. You find your rhythm, boosting earnings and savings for the future, steadily ascending the mountain.

During this phase, individuals become accustomed to market risks and stock volatility. Just like a climber preparing for unpredictable mountain weather, successful investors adeptly handle market fluctuations. This stage involves seeking capital growth by saving and venturing into riskier investments such as those available in 401Ks or employer retirement plans.

Over time, you witness the ebb and flow of the stock market—experiencing both bullish and bearish markets. Despite short-term market turbulence, the overarching trend remains upward. To navigate this landscape, one cultivates risk tolerance, understanding that downturns are often followed by recovery and growth.

The journey mirrors a climber's ascent, with challenges and adverse conditions along the way yet always leading upward. Remaining composed during market downturns, maintaining a long-term outlook, and staying resolute in your chosen path are key. This phase encapsulates the essence of the accumulation period, focusing on wealth growth, comfort with risk, and resilience to market fluctuations.

This zone represents the pivotal years during the Accumulation Phase. Your successful strategies involved maintaining a long-term perspective, staying committed, contributing to retirement accounts, automating investments, and ensuring you took enough risk to foster growth. Success in these endeavors has propelled you to heights you once only dreamed of reaching. With the mountain peak in view, you are now poised to venture into uncharted territory.

RETIREMENT ZONE 2: THE FINAL ASCENT—THE PRERETIREMENT ZONE

You're probably in *Zone 2* now, heading toward retirement. This starts as retirement approaches, typically between ages 50 and 65, when the idea of retirement shifts from a distant dream to a looming reality. This realization brings a mix of excitement and apprehension. While the freedom and self-direction of retirement is enticing, leaving behind a familiar routine and professional identity can be unsettling. Transitioning from a bustling career to retirement requires a significant shift in mindset and lifestyle. This period, termed the *Preretirement Zone*, is critical for reevaluating financial, emotional, and lifestyle plans.

As climbers on Everest brave the danger of their ultimate ascent, you now step into the financial *Danger Zone* with retirement approaching in about 5 years. Unlike your working years, when you could weather investment losses, time isn't as forgiving now. Your current strategies may fall short. The preretirement phase, the 5 years leading to retirement, resembles the final climb of a mountain. Strategic planning is crucial in this pivotal period, akin to the last push to the summit. It's not just about reaching the peak but also making wise decisions for a safe journey back.

Just as climbers assess their stamina, supplies, and weather conditions before the summit push, individuals nearing retirement must thoroughly review their financial situation. This includes evaluating savings, investments, and future retirement income sources to ensure readiness for postretirement life.

Similar to a climber's cautious approach during the final ascent, making rushed decisions or taking unnecessary risks in the preretirement phase can result in financial setbacks. Emotional and mental preparedness is key, as fatigue and excitement may cloud judgment. Choosing the right descent path is another critical decision.

Just as climbers brace themselves for the summit's elation and the challenge of the descent, individuals entering retirement must prepare for the emotional and psychological aspects of this life transition. Beyond financial readiness, readiness for a new lifestyle and identity in retirement sets the stage for a fulfilling post-career life. This zone marks the shift from the *Accumulation* to the *Distribution* phase, warranting special attention.

Success strategies in this zone involve crafting a withdrawal plan to secure retirement income and adjusting investment portfolios for effective risk management. Gradually shifting a portion of your savings to more stable assets can bolster financial stability, much like a climber cautiously choosing a safe descent route.

Beyond financial planning, you must prepare for lifestyle changes in retirement. Embrace hobbies, community engagement, part-time work, or volunteer opportunities to smoothen the transition, similar to climbers gearing up for the descent after summiting the peak.

This zone concludes as you approach your last day of work prior to retirement, signifying reaching the summit of the mountain climb.

RETIREMENT ZONE 3: THE SUMMIT—THE DAY OF RETIREMENT

This is the day you've been looking forward to—your retirement day! Reaching this peak parallels the exhilaration of summiting a mountain, a momentous achievement bringing immense joy and fulfillment. After years of toil, dedication, and meticulous planning, this milestone marks the triumphant conclusion of your career voyage. It's a time for celebration, reflection on past feats, and savoring the panoramic vista from the summit, the tangible outcome of your relentless labor.

The summit of your retirement day offers awe-inspiring vistas, embodying the freedom and possibilities retirement bestows. Yet, it also symbolizes financial uncertainties and forthcoming challenges, as it is the farthest point from the security of basecamp.

Similar to a climber embracing new horizons and obstacles at the summit, retirement heralds a fresh chapter rich with opportunities and obstacles. The newfound liberty of time is both liberating and intimidating. Abruptly, the framework and purpose of a career yields to a blank canvas. This paradigm shift offers profound fulfillment, inviting pursuit of interests, quality time with family, volunteering, or even embarking on a second career or entrepreneurial venture.

Conversely, it introduces fresh hurdles necessitating adaptation. The shift from earning and saving to spending and safeguarding may be disconcerting. Emotional and psychological adjustments are imperative as retirees seek novel ways to derive purpose and contentment each day. Just as a mountaineer meticulously plans their descent, retirees must strategize for this ensuing journey, ensuring they possess the resources—both financial and emotional—to relish a confident and enriching retirement. Truly, summiting is not a conclusion but the prelude to a thrilling new odyssey.

Much like mountaineering, where summiting is merely half the trek, retirement signifies a fresh commencement rather than a finale. Both mandate meticulous planning, informed choices, and unwavering perseverance to cultivate a gratifying and prosperous journey.

After this phase, you will move into the initial years of retirement covering the first decade. This period will demand new skills and financial management, as you will discover.

RETIREMENT ZONE 4: THE EARLY YEARS OF RETIREMENT—THE FIRST DECADE OF RETIREMENT

Having triumphed over the summit, the subsequent phase ushers in the early years of retirement and the launch of the distribution stage in retirement planning. This shift signifies a move from earning income through salaries to relying on savings and other retirement funds. It parallels the perilous beginning of the descent for mountain climbers, symbolizing the risky juncture of retirement. The initial decade is pivotal, requiring astute financial decisions and judicious adaptations to steer clear of major setbacks. Navigating this critical 10-year period without significant financial upheavals lays a sturdy groundwork for a confident retirement, resilient in the face of future challenges.

This phase presents the greatest challenge of all the *Retirement Zones* and necessitates utmost planning. Just as cautiously descending a mountain, managing resources wisely during this period is vital to safeguard the longevity of your savings. Though the descent lacks the thrill of the ascent, it is equally crucial in the quest for a prosperous retirement. By navigating this phase thoughtfully, retirees can safely maneuver through the *Danger Zone* and move confidently toward the subsequent chapter with security and assurance. The resilience cultivated and lessons absorbed during this time lay a solid foundation for a confident and fulfilling retirement, reflecting a climber's fortitude exhibited in a successful descent from Everest's perilous *Death Zone*.

Despite the intimidating aura of the *Danger Zone*, there is a silver lining. Successfully navigating the initial decade without financial setbacks paves the way for a smoother journey ahead. How can you not only endure but thrive throughout your entire retirement? It commences with understanding the significance of this pivotal moment. While this zone poses greater financial challenges than any other, it is arguably one of the most exhilarating times in your life. With health, energy, and resources at your disposal, you can pursue long-held desires such as travel, hobbies, and other interests. Thus, while demanding heightened financial attention, it also represents one of the finest opportunities to relish life.

Successful strategies in this phase involve securing the funds designated for immediate income during the initial 10 years alongside investing and expanding the funds allocated for future years. This delicate balance shields you during the critical first decade, which includes the *Danger Zone*, while also priming you for the years ahead. After the initial decade of retirement, you will have established a rhythm for your finances and lifestyle, now necessitating a slightly altered mindset.

RETIREMENT ZONE 5: THE STABILITY PHASE—NAVIGATING RETIREMENT BEYOND THE SECOND DECADE

Known as the *Stability Phase*, this stage of retirement life occurs in the second decade of retirement and thereafter. It embodies a period of consistent and harmonious living. The initial thrill of retirement gives way to a more tranquil existence as retirees acclimate to their new life chapter. It's a time when individuals concentrate on upholding their well-being, securing their finances for the long haul, and relishing their leisure time through hobbies, travel, or quality moments with loved ones.

After conquering the financial uncertainties of the summit and the first ten years of retirement, you can now exhale, much like a mountaineer who has passed the most perilous part of the climb. This phase of retirement presents an opportunity for individuals to savor the rewards of their hard work, akin to a climber admiring the awe-inspiring landscape during a safe descent. The worries about financial stability have evolved into feelings of safety and contentment, enabling retirees to focus on embracing their retirement to the fullest.

The *Stability Phase* of retirement ushers in a level of financial stability and predictability. Having fully transitioned from the active earning stage, retirees at this point have likely established spending habits that align with their retirement lifestyle. This firm grasp on their expenses allows for a reliable budget, reducing worries of financial strain and enhancing the enjoyment of their post-career years.

Additionally, during this phase, individuals typically have a refined financial management system in place. The adjustments made during the early retirement years have been fine-tuned, and they are now adept at effectively managing their assets and income sources. This involves maintaining a delicate equilibrium between essential expenses, desired leisure activities, and the establishment of emergency funds and investments for the future. This adept financial management fosters a sense of financial security and confidence, grounding their retired life with peace of mind.

These attributes of the *Stability Phase* underscore the significance of comprehensive financial planning and management throughout retirement. Just as a mountaineer's journey doesn't conclude after surpassing the *Danger Zone*, retirees must remain proactive and vigilant in overseeing their finances to help ensure that their retirement savings are resilient and substantial enough to uphold their desired lifestyle for years ahead.

USING THE RETIREMENT ZONES MODEL—NEARING RETIREMENT

Understanding the different stages of retirement is crucial for those on the brink of this significant life transition. Just as a mountaineer plans their route to the summit, individuals approaching retirement can gain substantial advantages by mapping out their retirement journey beforehand. This framework offers valuable perspectives on what to anticipate at each phase of retirement, helping individuals prepare for forthcoming changes and challenges.

Furthermore, the model underscores the psychological and emotional adjustments that come with each retirement zone, assisting individuals in preparing for the lifestyle shifts retirement brings. Thus, the model serves not only as a financial roadmap but also as a guide through the emotional facets of retirement, offering a comprehensive approach to retirement planning. By embracing and implementing this model, individuals readying for retirement can foresee and organize their retirement journey, ensuring a satisfying and more confident retirement.

In summary, the retirement passage is a multiphase adventure akin to a mountain ascent with its diverse terrains and obstacles. Just as each segment of a mountain climb necessitates distinct strategies and efforts, the retirement stages—encompassing working years, preretirement, retirement, the fragile first decade, and the stability phase—demand specific planning and management methods. Understanding and preparing for each phase can facilitate a seamless transition to a gratifying retirement. Similar to a climber reaching the summit and enjoying a safe descent, a retiree who has skillfully navigated these phases can relish the freedom and opportunities retirement offers, assured of their financial stability. Essentially, a well-planned retirement journey helps enable individuals to not only achieve their dreams but also relish the scenic route of their golden years.

If you're reading this book, chances are you've succeeded in Zone 1—the working years, and you're now nearing retirement, seeking guidance for what lay ahead. In the following section, I will discuss the *Retirement Traps*, the potential dangers in the retirement zones ahead. By understanding and preparing for these challenges today, you will be ready to face them when they arise.

PART II

THE TOP 10 RETIREMENT TRAPS

CHAPTER 4

RETIREMENT TRAP 1: THE LUCK FACTOR

THE PRECARIOUS TRANSITION TO RETIREMENT

As you approach retirement, a significant financial risk looms large, posing a threat to your financial stability. This risk emerges as you near retirement and persists during the initial decade post-retirement. It represents the primary challenge during this *Danger Zone*, akin to climbers facing their toughest trials on the final ascent to Mount Everest's peak and the first part of the descent.

I refer to this looming risk as the *Luck Factor*, symbolizing the unpredictability of investment and economic performance during the pivotal years leading up to your retirement and the first decade in retirement. If you're unprepared for unexpected financial shocks, including a significant stock market downturn, a recession, or a financial crisis occurring just before or after your retirement, you may face challenging circumstances. The anticipation of retirement can be filled with hope, but potential substantial loss of savings could leave you vulnerable unless you're ready for such scenarios.

BRACING FOR THE UNCONTROLLABLE

Similar to how climbers brace for unpredictable weather, retirees must acknowledge the uncontrollable elements of this risk. That's why it's known as the *Luck Factor*—regardless of who you are or what you believe, you lack control over these elements. The timing of the performance of the stock market and the economy when you plan to retire depends purely on luck. All you can do is prepare. Although you cannot influence market performance or economic conditions, unexpected financial challenges at the beginning of retirement may present difficulties.

UNDERSTANDING THE LUCK FACTOR

Understanding the *Luck Factor* is critical. In financial planning circles, this may also be referenced as the *Sequence of Returns Risk*. The essence of this risk lay in the timing of poor investment returns or economic conditions, which, if they occur at the cusp of retirement or during early retirement years could drastically undermine your financial stability. Analogous to climbers on Everest, you may find yourself depleting your resources more rapidly than anticipated to weather a financial storm. The aftermath may leave you with insufficient reserves to enjoy the entirety of your retirement.

Bracing to withstand the *Luck Factor* requires a shift from the strategies of the accumulation phase, where the focus is on long-term investment returns regardless of annual performance fluctuations. While that strategy may fare well during the working years, the retirement phase demands a more nuanced approach. The sequence in which you experience investment returns can significantly impact the longevity of your retirement savings. Early losses can have a more profound effect than those occurring later in retirement due to the compounded consequence of withdrawing funds on a depreciated portfolio.

THE SHORTCOMINGS OF SUSTAINABLE WITHDRAWAL RATES

Many retirement income strategies, including the popular *Sustainable Withdrawal Rate* approach, do not adequately address the risks of the *Luck Factor*. Without careful planning, retirees adhering to the 4% or 5% rule may witness their savings dwindle alarmingly fast, potentially depleting their nest egg prematurely. Imagine the anxiety of watching your life savings diminish during the initial years of retirement. Such a scenario is not only stressful but could lead to years of living in fear over the next economic downturn.

STRATEGIZING AGAINST THE LUCK FACTOR

Therefore, it's imperative to devise a well-thought-out strategy that mitigates the *Luck Factor* for the funds you need in the short term while ensuring the potential growth of resources intended for later use. This demonstrates that investment strategies effective during the accumulation phase may not necessarily benefit you in the distribution phase. This highlights the need for dynamic financial planning that evolves to meet the distinct needs of each phase in your financial life. Understanding and planning for the *Luck Factor* can make all the difference between a retirement spent in financial confidence or one filled with uncertainty. Equip yourself with the knowledge and strategies needed to traverse this *Danger Zone*, helps ensure a stable and prosperous journey through your retirement years.

SUMMARY OF TRAP 1: THE LUCK FACTOR

- Poor investment returns or losses during the first decade of retirement may severely impact your financial well-being, especially if you are depending on your investments for income.
- The sequence in which you experience investment returns plays a critical role in the overall health of your retirement savings.

- Experiencing negative returns early in retirement can have a lasting detrimental effect, altering the course of your retirement years.
- This risk predominantly affects individuals nearing retirement or those who have recently retired and are relying on their investments to generate income.
- The timing of returns often holds more significance than the magnitude of the returns themselves in determining the success of your retirement income strategy.

CHAPTER 5

RETIREMENT TRAP 2: LONGEVITY RISK IN RETIREMENT PLANNING

INTRODUCTION TO LONGEVITY RISK

In this chapter, we'll delve into a significant risk that emerges in the later stages of retirement. While this topic often sparks anxiety, meticulous planning and strategic thinking can help you steer clear of this pitfall. The universal aspiration for a long and fulfilling life necessitates prudent financial management to help ensure that your resources align with your longevity. A great way to begin is by delving into your potential lifespan.

THE REALITY OF MODERN LIFESPANS

Most individuals stepping into their early 60s should brace themselves for a retirement that could span 30-35 years. This necessitates a financial strategy robust enough to sustain both themselves and their spouses until at least the age of 95. The notion of preparing for such an extended time frame may feel overly cautious to some, yet in an era marked by rapid advancements in medical technology, extending one's life expectancy by a decade or more than current projections is not just possible—it's becoming increasingly probable. Studies such as those conducted by the London School of Business affirm this trend by highlighting that the average life expectancy has risen by approximately three years every decade in recent history.

STATISTICAL PROBABILITIES AND RETIREMENT PLANNING

Consider the statistical probabilities of current longevity projections for a moment. For a married couple both aged 65, there's a fifty percent chance that one will live to at least age 94. And for individuals, the odds of reaching into the late 80s to early 90s are equally compelling. These figures illustrate that planning for life into one's mid-90s is not only realistic but essential.

PERSONALIZING YOUR FINANCIAL STRATEGY

It's critical to understand that you cannot solely depend on the patterns of your ancestry to guide your financial planning for longevity. Genetic predisposition does play a role in life expectancy, but it's just one part. Equally, relying on average life expectancy figures—a median within a vast spectrum of the population—is inadequate for personal financial planning. Your strategy should account for the possibility of reaching age 95 or beyond, unless there is compelling evidence suggesting that both you or your spouse will not attain such longevity.

THE CONSEQUENCES OF FAILING TO PLAN

Failing to plan for longevity can have serious consequences. Depleting your savings in retirement may force you into compromising your lifestyle and lowering your quality of life. It is crucial to approach retirement planning realistically by considering your potential lifespan. Assuming only an 80-year life expectancy and spending accordingly is risky, overlooking advancements in healthcare and increased longevity. This could result in needing support from family members or selling assets such as your home to make ends meet, which may not be ideal.

SUMMARY OF TRAP 2: *LONGEVITY RISK*

- Planning for retirement must account for the likelihood of living beyond traditional life expectancy, potentially up to or beyond the age of 95 due to advancements in medical technology and increased average lifespans.

- A robust financial strategy is crucial for ensuring that one's financial resources do not deplete over a retirement phase that could last 30-35 years.
- Reliance on historical or familial patterns of life expectancy is inadequate for modern retirement planning. A conservative approach that considers the possibility of living to 95 or beyond is essential.
- The failure to plan for extended longevity may lead to significant financial strain, lifestyle compromises, and a reduced quality of life in one's later years.

CHAPTER 6

RETIREMENT TRAP 3: INFLATION

This chapter is dedicated to unraveling the complexities of inflation, illuminating its core characteristics and its dual role in the economic landscape. It offers valuable insights into managing its impact on personal finances, especially during retirement. While you've been in the workforce, inflation has not been a major worry. In fact, the peak of your career coincided with a period of historically low and stable inflation rates. Only recently has inflation captured widespread attention.

UNDERSTANDING INFLATION

Inflation is a pervasive economic phenomenon indicative of a steady increase in living costs. It stands as a silent yet potent force capable of diminishing purchasing power over time if not properly addressed in financial planning. Surprisingly, inflation has been a consistent presence in our economic landscape, an unwavering factor amidst fluctuating market dynamics since 1926, with an average annual inflation rate of approximately 3%. Despite this, periods such as the 1970s witnessed higher rates averaging around 8%, showcasing the variable nature of inflation through different economic eras.

THE DUAL NATURE OF INFLATION

It's crucial to recognize that inflation's implications are not universally viewed through a negative lens. Many economists argue that an inflation rate hovering around 2% signifies a robust and thriving economy. This perspective is further reinforced by the U.S. Federal Reserve, which envisions a 2% inflation rate as optimal for economic health. In essence, inflation emerges as a consequence of economic growth driven by an uptick in consumer purchasing that often surpasses supply capacities. This imbalance between demand and supply acts as a catalyst, compelling producers to escalate prices and thus perpetuating the cycle of economic activity.

THE HIDDEN DANGERS OF PRICE DECREASES—DEFLATION

Conversely, dismissing inflation in hopes of its disappearance is ill-advised since its antithesis, deflation, poses even greater risks to economic stability. Deflation, characterized by a persistent dip in demand, instigates a downward spiral of prices, curtails production, and can precipitate unemployment, entrenching the economy in a state of lethargy.

Inflation remains a consistent element within our financial system, a factor that persists and demands attention. Failure to address it adequately in your plans may lead to detrimental impacts on your quality of life. Let's explore its potential effects on a retiree's income.

INFLATION'S IMPACT ON QUALITY OF LIFE

Beyond its immediate impact, the long-term effects of inflation are profound, particularly on personal financial landscapes. To illustrate, envision retiring at age 60 with an annual income of $100,000. Should inflation persist at an average rate of 3% for the subsequent 15 years, your purchasing power equivalent to your first retirement year would plummet to $63,000, marking a staggering 37% decrease. Such a scenario underscores the imperative of incorporating inflation into financial planning to safeguard financial resources and maintain a desired standard of living post-retirement.

STRATEGIC MITIGATION OF INFLATION

Strategies such as introducing a *Cost of Living Adjustment* (COLA) of around 2-3% and directing financial resources to investments that outpace inflation can help mitigate its negative impact. Recognizing and planning for inflation is crucial for sustaining quality of life amidst economic shifts.

SUMMARY OF KEY POINTS

- **INFLATION DEFINED:** Inflation is an economic condition marked by an ongoing increase in the cost of living, reducing purchasing power over time. It has been a constant element of the economic landscape, averaging an annual rate of approximately 3% since 1926, though significantly higher rates have been experienced in certain periods such as the 1970s.
- **DUAL NATURE OF INFLATION**: While often perceived negatively due to its diminishment of purchasing power, inflation is also seen by many economists as a sign of a healthy economy, especially when the rate hovers around 2%, as this indicates a level of economic growth and vitality.
- **RISKS OF IGNORING INFLATION**: The chapter highlights the dangers of overlooking inflation or wishing for its disappearance, as its counterpart, deflation, can lead to worse economic conditions, including decreased demand, falling prices, reduced production, and increased unemployment.

- **LONG-TERM IMPACTS ON PERSONAL FINANCE**: Notably, inflation profoundly affects personal finances over the long term, significantly reducing one's purchasing power in retirement if not strategically planned for. An example given elucidates how a $100,000 income could effectively decrease in value by 37% over 15 years due to a 3% average inflation rate.
- **MITIGATION STRATEGIES**: To combat inflation's effects, the chapter suggests incorporating a *Cost of Living Adjustment* (COLA) of about 2-3% and investing in vehicles that are likely to outpace inflation. These strategies are essential for preserving financial resources, ensuring a sustained quality of life, and achieving more financial confidence in the face of economic changes.

CHAPTER 7

RETIREMENT TRAP 4: AN INADEQUATE INVESTMENT STRATEGY

In the realm of personal finance and retirement planning, the word *strategy* carries an air of mystique, often equated with complexity and critical importance. Yet at its heart, a strategy is nothing more than a coherent plan devised to achieve a set goal. This principle holds true particularly in the sphere of investments. At the core of any investment strategy lies a profound understanding of risk—recognizing when to avoid it and how to harness it to work in your favor under the right circumstances. The choices you make regarding your investments and the overarching strategy you adopt can significantly influence your risk level.

THE TRANSITION OF STRATEGIES FROM ACCUMULATION TO DISTRIBUTION

During the accumulation phase leading up to retirement, the primary aim is to amass as much capital as possible. Naturally, your strategy during this period gravitates towards aggressive savings and investments. However, upon entering retirement, the game changes. Your focus should pivot to preserving your accumulated wealth, generating sustainable income from it while simultaneously ensuring its growth. This shift necessitates adopting a strategy that is balanced and nuanced, tailored to the unique demands of retirement.

THE PENDULUM SWING OF RETIREMENT STRATEGIES

Observation reveals that upon retiring, many individuals find themselves vacillating between two extremes. Some cling to the aggressive investment strategies of their preretirement years, while others shift to an overly conservative approach. Both extremes can lead to a misjudgment of risk and the potentially poor outcomes. Instead, I propose a retirement-centric strategy that steers clear of extremes—a balanced approach that recognizes the varying timeframes for different portions of your retirement funds. Some funds needed in the near future should be safeguarded against excessive risk. Meanwhile, funds earmarked for later use can afford to bear a higher level of risk.

RISK TOLERANCE VS RISK AWARENESS

Understanding the dichotomy between risk tolerance and risk awareness is crucial. Risk tolerance corresponds to your personal comfort level with investment risk, while risk awareness pertains to recognizing the level of risk required to meet your objectives. Decisions grounded solely in risk tolerance may result in taking on excessive risks or, conversely, stagnation and the potential erosion of your capital.

A TRAVEL ANALOGY FOR INVESTMENT STRATEGY

Consider a travel scenario: You take a travel preference assessment that indicates a fondness for slow travel such as a slow-moving cruise. However, your destination is Australia, you live in the United States, and time is limited. Despite your preference for slower modes of transport, the circumstances necessitate taking a flight—the fastest means to reach your destination. You may find yourself wanting to know more about air travel—its risks, rewards, and costs—but eventually you come to understand that it's the most effective way to reach your destination. This logic is applicable to investments, as well. Understanding the *why* and *how* of risk-taking offers a clearer roadmap for your necessary investment strategy.

Understanding the underlying principles of risk-taking will provide a clearer roadmap for navigating the financial landscape of investing in retirement.

THE ROAD AHEAD

To summarize, it is paramount to develop a robust investment strategy for retirement. Such a strategy should carefully balance risk management to preserve and grow your capital. Relying solely on preretirement strategies or flipping to an excessively conservative stance can mismanage risk. Recognizing the different investment time horizons for portions of your retirement funds and balancing risk tolerance with risk awareness is key. The principle that some risks are necessary to achieve your financial goals, much like the need to board a plane to reach distant shores swiftly, is fundamental to navigating the complexities of retirement investing.

SUMMARY OF KEY POINTS:

- **UNDERSTAND THE NATURE OF STRATEGY:** A successful investment strategy is a coherent plan aimed at achieving specific financial goals. It involves a crucial understanding of risk and making informed decisions to manage it effectively.
- **TRANSITIONING STRATEGIES AT RETIREMENT:** The shift from the accumulation phase to the distribution phase necessitates a change in investment strategy, moving from aggressive capital growth to a focus on wealth preservation and income generation.

- **AVOID EXTREMES IN RETIREMENT STRATEGY:** A balanced investment approach in retirement is vital. Avoid sticking strictly to preretirement aggressive strategies or shifting to an overly conservative stance. Tailor your strategy to manage risks appropriately for different time horizons of your retirement funds.
- **RISK TOLERANCE VS RISK AWARENESS:** It's important to distinguish between your personal comfort level with risk (risk tolerance) and the level of risk needed to meet your financial objectives (risk awareness). Decisions should be made based on a comprehensive understanding of both.
- **THE IMPORTANCE OF RISK IN ACHIEVING GOALS:** Similar to choosing the fastest mode of transport to swiftly reach a distant destination, some risks are necessary to achieve long-term financial objectives. Understanding why and how to take calculated risks is essential in developing a robust retirement investment strategy.

CHAPTER 8

RETIREMENT TRAP 5: SPENDING TOO MUCH

In the landscape of retirement planning, a crucial challenge arises—the danger of overdrawing from savings. This chapter endeavors to illuminate the consequences of such oversights and imparts wisdom on navigating this potential retirement trap with prudence.

THE REALITY OF RETIREMENT SPENDING

Retirement, a period envisioned for tranquility and fulfillment, can quickly devolve into financial turmoil when retirees indulge in excessive withdrawals from their nest egg. This isn't a mere consequence of lavish spending or poor budgeting. Instead, it's often the result of over-optimistic and incorrect assumptions regarding the sustainable withdrawal rate and the growth rates of their investments.

THE DANGER OF MISPLACED OPTIMISM

Many retirees, driven by a misguided belief in perpetual high investment returns, set themselves down a precarious path. They overlook the unpredictable nature of market dynamics, which can fluctuate dramatically and affect their financial stability. Even with a meticulously planned budget, erroneous assumptions about withdrawal rates and investment returns can precipitate the premature erosion of one's financial reserves.

THE ILLUSION OF MARKET DEPENDENCE

This phenomenon forces retirees into an uneasy dependence on the stock market's performance for their financial sustenance. Herein lies a vital lesson—the essence of security in retirement finances lay in grounding your financial strategies on realistic expectations concerning investment returns and judicious management of income withdrawals.

QUESTIONING *THE 4% RULE*

One of the flawed paradigms in this context is the *4% Rule*—an ostensibly simple strategy that suggests withdrawing 4% of your retirement savings annually. Its allure lay in its simplicity; however, it dangerously disregards individual nuances and the vicissitudes of market behavior. Such simplifications assume consistent investment returns—a scenario far removed from the erratic reality of financial markets. Furthermore, by adopting a generalized approach, the *4% Rule* fails to accommodate personal variables that significantly influence sustainable withdrawal rates, such as health, life expectancy, and other income sources.

TOWARD A MORE INFORMED APPROACH

Conclusively, while heuristic rules such as the *4% Rule* offer the seduction of simplicity, they may inadvertently pave the way to financial distress for many retirees. The realm of retirement financing is inherently complex, sculpted by personal circumstances, lifestyle aspirations, and the whims of market forces. Therefore, ensuring a more confident and fulfilling retirement necessitates the adoption of informed, nuanced assumptions in determining your withdrawal strategy. This chapter aims to highlight this critical aspect of retirement planning, bolstering your financial acumen.

SUMMARY OF KEY POINTS

- **UNDERSTANDING THE RISK OF OVERDRAWING**: Retirees often underestimate the peril of drawing too much from their retirement savings, endangering their financial stability due to optimistic assumptions about the market and withdrawal rates.

- **THE CONSEQUENCES OF OVER-OPTIMISM**: By relying on unrealistic expectations of perpetual high returns, retirees may face premature depletion of their funds, becoming overly dependent on the fluctuating stock market for their livelihood.
- **CHALLENGING THE *4% RULE***: The simplicity of the *4% Rule*—withdrawing 4% of retirement savings yearly—ignores individual circumstances and market volatility, often leading to financial insecurity.
- **THE IMPORTANCE OF REALISTIC PLANNING**: A more confident retirement is built on realistic assumptions about investment returns and careful income withdrawal management, adjusting strategies to accommodate market changes and personal needs.
- **NAVIGATING RETIREMENT WITHDRAWALS WISELY**: Ensuring a fulfilling retirement requires moving beyond simplifications such as the *4% Rule* to adopt informed, nuanced withdrawal strategies that consider personal circumstances and the unpredictable nature of financial markets.

CHAPTER 9

RETIREMENT TRAP 6: HEALTHCARE COSTS

Retirement, often envisioned as a time of freedom and relief from work-related stress, brings its own set of challenges, especially in managing healthcare expenses. Many retirees worry about rising healthcare costs as they grow older. This section delves into the complexities of these expenses and provides strategies for effective management.

LONG-TERM CARE COSTS

A glaring issue in the landscape of retirement healthcare costs is the expense associated with long-term care. Ranging from simple assistance with daily activities to comprehensive medical supervision in a nursing facility, the costs are often underappreciated, and the common belief that Medicare will cover these expenses is unfortunately a misconception. This reality brings to light the limitations of Medicare, which does not extend to long-term care, and Medicaid's assistance kicks in only after one's personal assets have significantly dwindled.

To combat the potential financial upheaval this could cause, it's imperative to adopt a strategic approach. Options such as purchasing long-term care insurance, allocating a portion of savings specifically for this purpose, or exploring alternative care solutions can prove to be substantial in averting a financial crisis stemming from long-term care expenses.

UNDERSTANDING MEDICARE

Medicare, the beacon of hope for many retirees, does cater to a significant chunk of healthcare needs. However, the specifics of what it covers (and what falls outside its purview) must be thoroughly understood to prevent unexpected financial burdens. Notably, while it encompasses expenses like hospital stays and some home healthcare, it stops short of covering long-term care, specific prescription drugs, and routine dental or vision care.

Another aspect worth highlighting is the distinction in costs associated with Medicare Part A, usually free for those who have contributed to the system through their work, and Part B, which carries a standard premium of $174.70 per month as of 2024, with potential increases based on income levels.

EMERGENCY HEALTHCARE COSTS

The unpredictability of life underscores the importance of being financially prepared for health emergencies. Such events can impose substantial costs and, without proper planning, may severely deplete one's retirement savings. Incorporating a financial buffer within the retirement budget dedicated to covering unforeseen medical expenses is a prudent strategy. It not only provides a much-needed safety net but also contributes to peace of mind, safeguarding against the financial impact of unexpected health crises.

In conclusion, the path to a financially confident and enjoyable retirement is intricately linked with the ability to adeptly manage healthcare costs. Equipped with a deep understanding of these expenses and a strategic plan of action, retirees can look forward to savoring their golden years free from the shadow of financial worry.

SUMMARY OF KEY POINTS

- Long-term healthcare potentially represents a substantial expense in retirement, requiring careful planning and consideration. Solutions include long-term care insurance, dedicated savings, or exploring alternative care avenues.
- A comprehensive understanding of Medicare's coverage scope and premium costs is essential for financial planning in retirement. The standard

monthly premium for Part B in 2024 is $174.70, with adjustments based on income.

- The unpredictable nature of health emergencies necessitates a financial buffer within the retirement budget, ensuring readiness and resources to address unforeseen medical expenses, thus facilitating a stress-free retirement experience.

CHAPTER 10

RETIREMENT TRAP 7: FINANCIAL SHOCKS

FINANCIAL SHOCKS IN RETIREMENT

The significance of financial stability in retirement cannot be overstated. Being prepared for unexpected financial shocks is paramount, as these can significantly impact the quality of life in your golden years. The possibility of a market downturn, sudden medical expenses, or even the need for long-term care are just a few examples of unanticipated expenses that can derail your retirement plans. By prioritizing the reliability and flexibility of your income sources, you can build a financial buffer against these potential shocks. This may include strategies such as keeping a portion of your investments in low-risk, easily accessible assets, or maintaining an emergency fund specifically for unexpected expenses. In essence, being prepared for financial shocks is not merely about survival but ensuring the sustainability and stability of your lifestyle throughout retirement.

FREQUENCY OF FINANCIAL SHOCKS IN RETIREMENT

Financial shocks in retirement are not uncommon. Rather, they are a prevalent occurrence. Research indicates that a significant portion of retirees encounter at least one financial shock, and some face multiple shocks throughout their retirement years. Given the high likelihood of unexpected expenses, it becomes even more critical to have flexible, reliable, and stable income sources in retirement, along with adequate reserves. These income sources and reserves act as a safety net, allowing retirees to weather financial storms without compromising their overall retirement plans and lifestyle. By prioritizing these safeguards, retirees protect themselves against unforeseen challenges and maintain their financial well-being.

EXAMPLES OF FINANCIAL SHOCKS IN RETIREMENT

1. **HEALTHCARE COSTS:** One of the most common financial shocks in retirement are unexpected healthcare costs. These can stem from sudden medical emergencies, chronic illnesses, or the need for long-term care—expenses that are often

underestimated and can significantly deplete retirement savings.

2. **FAMILY EMERGENCIES:** Financial shocks can also arise from family emergencies, such as needing to financially support a grown child facing economic issues or contributing to the care of aging parents.
3. **UNEXPECTED HOME REPAIRS:** Homeowners may encounter unexpected expenses related to significant home repairs or maintenance, such as a new roof or HVAC system, which can pose a substantial financial burden.

FINANCIAL RESERVES—PROTECTION AGAINST FINANCIAL SHOCKS

Retirement should be a time of peace, enjoyment, and fulfillment. However, without proper planning, individuals may find themselves facing stress instead of serenity. A critical component of a robust retirement plan is the establishment of a reserve or emergency fund sometimes called a *Rainy Day fund.* This fund acts as a financial safeguard, providing an extra layer of protection when unforeseen expenses emerge. It's essential for this fund to be maintained separately from other investments, particularly those designated for generating income, to help ensure its availability in times of need.

In the beginning of this book, you may have gathered from the quote from President Eisenhower that I have an interest for reading and extracting lessons from military history. One valuable lesson linked to the significance of reserves stems from the wisdom of Napoleon Bonaparte, a renowned military strategist. Napoleon comprehended the essence of warfare and the essential role of strategic reserves. He notably stressed the necessity of retaining a segment of his troops in reserve, refraining from simultaneously deploying all his forces at the frontline. This approach enabled him to adjust to the fluidity of battle, react to unforeseen circumstances, and exploit gaps in the enemy's defense. By holding back troops, Napoleon could bolster weak areas, launch crucial counterattacks, or pursue retreating enemies, ultimately shifting the outcomes of numerous engagements in his favor. This strategy not only showcases tactical brilliance but also reveals a deep understanding of the unpredictable nature of combat—a parallel that can be drawn to life's uncertainties in retirement. The ability to swiftly adapt to new situations and exhibit flexibility often determines the victor in both warfare and life's challenges.

SUMMARY OF KEY POINTS

- **PREPARATION FOR FINANCIAL SHOCKS:** It's crucial to anticipate and prepare for potential financial shocks in retirement, such as market downturns, unexpected healthcare costs, and sudden home repairs, to maintain a high quality of life.

- **RELIABILITY AND FLEXIBILITY OF INCOME SOURCES:** Having diverse, reliable, and flexible income sources, along with reserves, acts as a safeguard, enabling retirees to handle financial emergencies without compromising their standard of living.
- **COMMON FINANCIAL SHOCKS:** The most prevalent financial shocks in retirement include high healthcare costs, family emergencies requiring financial support, and significant, unforeseen home maintenance expenses.
- **CONSEQUENCES OF UNPREPAREDNESS:** Without preparation, financial shocks can deplete savings rapidly, lead to enhanced stress, and in severe cases, forces retirees into a drastic lifestyle downgrade or to reenter the workforce.

CHAPTER 11

RETIREMENT TRAP 8: MAKING EMOTIONAL DECISIONS ABOUT MONEY

INTRODUCTION TO BEHAVIORAL FINANCE

In the pursuit of financial wisdom, one must traverse the intricate landscape of *Behavioral Finance*. This intriguing domain, nestled at the crossroads of psychology and economics, endeavors to unravel a perplexing enigma—the propensity of individuals to make suboptimal monetary choices often driven by emotions despite possessing adequate financial insight.

Behavioral Finance posits a compelling narrative about the human condition— we are, more often than not, our own worst adversaries in money management. This predicament doesn't stem from a lack of knowledge or competence but rather from our brain's hardwired inclination to perceive financial loss as a palpable threat. Triggered by the limbic system, this primordial fight-or-flight reflex can precipitate swift, emotionally charged reactions during times of financial stress such as market downturns, leading to precipitate decisions about investments that are usually to our detriment.

The revelation of our brain's default reaction underscores the importance of developing strategies to temper these emotional impulses. Thus, mastering the principles of *Behavioral Finance* equips us with the power to mitigate our instinctual responses.

ROLE OF COGNITIVE BIASES

Central to the dilemmas of even the most financially savvy individuals are two predominant behavioral biases: loss aversion and overconfidence. Loss aversion elucidates our psychological predisposition to fear potential losses more intensely than we value equivalent gains, creating a tumultuous balance between caution and ambition and often deterring us from accepting even reasonable levels of risk. Conversely, overconfidence emerges from an exaggerated confidence in our personal abilities and knowledge, enticing us to take unwarranted risks under the illusion of control and foresight, thereby underestimating potential dangers and overestimating returns.

STRATEGIES TO COUNTER COGNITIVE BIASES

The key to overcoming these cognitive distortions lies in acknowledging them and systematically countering their influences. By grasping the emotional and cognitive biases that impact our choices, we can develop strategies to mitigate their impact. These approaches include seeking unbiased financial guidance, following a structured decision-making process, and regularly reviewing our financial plans and assumptions.

SUMMARY OF KEY POINTS

- *Behavioral Finance* melds psychology with economics to decode the irrational financial decisions driven by cognitive biases and emotional responses. The predominant biases impacting financial choices include loss aversion, overconfidence, and confirmation bias.
- These biases prompt emotional reactions that culminate in less-than-ideal financial decisions, such as clinging to unprofitable investments, engaging in excessive risk, and biased decision-making due to confirmation bias. They pose formidable barriers to effective financial management.

- Countering these biases involves their recognition, comprehension of their effects, and the execution of strategies to mitigate their impact. Strategies include obtaining independent financial counsel, employing a structured decision-making protocol, and consistently evaluating financial plans and assumptions. With awareness and strategic actions, these biases can be transformed from adversaries into allies in financial decision-making. Overall, acquiring knowledge about *Behavioral Finance* empowers individuals to navigate their mind's maze and make sound financial choices despite the influence of cognitive biases.

CHAPTER 12

RETIREMENT TRAP 9: FAILING TO PLAN FOR TAXES IN RETIREMENT

UNDERSTANDING TAXATION OF RETIREMENT INCOME

Retirement marks a significant transition, not just in terms of lifestyle but also when managing personal finances. A crucial aspect that often catches retirees off guard is the complex terrain of taxes. This chapter sheds light on understanding and effectively managing taxes, ensuring that your golden years remain golden, financially speaking.

When it comes to managing your finances in retirement, a key aspect to consider is how different sources of income are taxed. Income from tax-deferred sources, such as IRA or 401K accounts, is subject to regular income tax rates, while income from other sources may be taxed at capital gains rates or could be exempt from further taxation if taxes have been previously paid.

THE IRS: YOUR UNAVOIDABLE "SILENT PARTNER"

As you plan your retirement, you'll need to consider the Internal Revenue Service (IRS) as your "Silent Partner." Any profits, dividends, or withdrawals from tax-deferred accounts will inevitably require a payment to your silent partner. Depending on your total income, 50% to 85% of your Social Security income may also be taxable.

While the thought of managing the impact of taxes is tempting, there is no magic formula that legally allows you to avoid all tax on your retirement income. The best approach is to strategically manage your finances to avoid sudden tax shocks. Most strategies offered by financial news outlets often yield empty results. For example, Roth Conversions, where a portion of a Traditional IRA is converted into a Roth IRA, still require payment of taxes at the time of conversion. While there are many proposed tactics available, some are unrealistic and should be approached with caution.

If you have funds only in a traditional IRA or tax deferred account, the plan is straightforward—your retirement income will come from these sources, and you'll pay regular income taxes at the federal level and potentially state taxes, as well, depending on your state's laws.

If your money is in a nonretirement or taxable account, you'll pay annual taxes on dividends and taxable interest produced, and capital gains taxes on investments held for at least a year, have a gain, and are sold. This necessitates careful planning, particularly for investments generating long-term capital gains.[1]

BLENDING YOUR INCOME SOURCES TO MANAGE TAXES

Strategically combining your income sources is key to optimizing your tax situation. For example, if you have a tax-deferred IRA and a non-qualified brokerage account, withdrawing equal amounts from both can help balance tax implications. This approach allows you to split your income between regular rates and potentially lower capital gains rates or even tax-free scenarios, leveraging the benefits of each. This straightforward approach to combining income can be tailored to your specific circumstances for efficient tax liability management.

Remember that from age 73, Required Minimum Distributions (RMDs) from your IRA become mandatory.

---

1 Converting an employer plan account or Traditional IRA to a Roth IRA is a taxable event. Increased taxable income from the Roth IRA conversion may have several consequences including but not limited to, a need for additional tax withholding or estimated tax payments, the loss of certain tax deductions and credits, and higher taxes on Social Security benefits and higher Medicare premiums. Be sure to consult with a qualified tax advisor before making any decisions regarding your IRA.

It may be beneficial to start using your IRA before this to avoid abruptly swerving from tax-free or lower-tax income to taxable income. This can shield you from unexpected tax burdens and help maintain your income at a level that doesn't disqualify you from certain deductions or increase your Medicare premiums.

TAXES IN RETIREMENT

Remember that taxes don't disappear in retirement. Understanding taxation is critical as you plan for this phase of your life. There isn't a magical one-size-fits-all solution, but there are guidelines that can be useful to follow.

One important point to remember is not to exhaust all your taxable accounts first while withholding usage of your IRAs. Doing so may result in significantly larger RMDs later in life, thereby increasing your tax burden. Keeping your taxable income low can also prevent increases in Medicare premiums and other associated costs.

SUMMARY OF KEY POINTS

- Managing taxes in retirement is critical, and understanding the tax implications of different income sources can help retirees blend their income streams effectively. Careful planning can prevent sudden spikes in taxable income, ensuring that retirees do not lose out on certain deductions or face increased Medicare premiums.

- Financial institutions can withhold taxes from income payouts, simplifying the day-to-day management of tax payments and freeing up retirees' time. Retirees, however, must perceive the IRS as an unavoidable "silent partner" that will consistently receive their share. Thus, no strategy can completely eliminate taxes on retirement income.
- If the bulk of a retiree's funds are in a traditional IRA or deferred account, they will be taxed at regular rates at both federal and potentially state levels. Assets in non-retirement or taxable accounts will incur annual taxes on gains and dividends. It's crucial not to deplete all taxable accounts before using IRAs, as this could lead to larger Required Minimum Distributions (RMDs) later in life, increasing the tax burden.

CHAPTER 13

RETIREMENT TRAP 10: OVERINDULGING IN NEWS AND MEDIA

It's crucial to recognize that the media doesn't always align with your financial retirement goals. News sources often sensationalize headlines and propagate fear-based narratives, potentially leading to poor financial choices.

Excessive media consumption may also introduce unnecessary stress during retirement. Retirees should minimize exposure to news outlets and focus on positive activities such as spending time with loved ones and pursuing hobbies.

EFFECTS OF MEDIA CONSUMPTION AND FEAR

I've observed many recent retirees dedicate more time to staying informed and entertained through increased news consumption. Whether through traditional news channels, websites, or social media, these typically composed individuals have shown heightened concerns about issues they hadn't previously discussed with me. This change seems to stem from increased media exposure. Unchecked, these retirees may start believing in a world in constant crisis, leading to anxiety about their investments and impulsive, emotionally driven decisions.

THE CONSEQUENCES OF EXCESSIVE MEDIA INTAKE

In today's digital age, staying informed is effortless. However, consuming excessive news may amplify stress, especially in retirement when leisure time is abundant. Continuous exposure to negative news may affect mental well-being, resulting in heightened anxiety, stress, and even sleep disturbances. Earlier, we explored the risks of emotional decision-making influenced by media-induced reactions that hinder rational choices.

BALANCING MEDIA CONSUMPTION FOR PERSONAL AND FINANCIAL WELL-BEING

Maintaining a healthy equilibrium involves managing media intake wisely. Limit daily news consumption by allocating specific time slots for this activity. Choose reliable news sources to avoid sensational content that induces stress. Your emotional and financial health are likely to benefit from reduced exposure to fear-inducing news.

PRIORITIZE QUALITY INFORMATION

Stay informed without compromising your mental and financial stability. In retirement, it's crucial to strike a balance between staying updated and avoid media overload. Focus on enriching content that enhances your life rather than overwhelming yourself with excessive information.

UNDERSTANDING NEWS CONSUMPTION REALITIES

Remember that news outlets prioritize viewership over your well-being or informed decision-making. Their main goal is selling ad space, often favoring sensationalized stories to retain your attention. Stay mindful of your information sources and intake levels.

PERSONAL INSIGHTS ON RETIREMENT AND MEDIA

I've personally witnessed retirees consuming more news post-retirement, perceiving an endless stream of crises. They discuss these issues as if they're newly urgent despite the world remaining relatively unchanged. The heightened exposure to news events and media sensationalism drives this perception shift.

SUMMARY OF KEY POINTS

- **IMPACT ON MENTAL HEALTH**: Excessive consumption of news and media, particularly negative news, may significantly impact mental well-being, causing increased anxiety, stress, and sleep issues, especially during retirement.
- **STRATEGIES FOR MANAGING CONSUMPTION**: To promote mental health and well-being, it's important to limit the time spent on media consumption by scheduling specific times for engaging with news and choosing reliable sources to avoid sensationalism.
- **IMPORTANCE OF QUALITY OVER QUANTITY**: Staying informed is crucial, but not at the expense of one's mental health. In retirement, it's essential to focus on consuming content that enriches life and avoids information overload.
- **UNDERSTANDING MEDIA MOTIVES**: News outlets aim to attract large viewership primarily to sell advertising space, often using sensationalized stories. It's vital to be discerning about the sources of information and the amount consumed.
- **OBSERVATIONS ON RETIREMENT AND NEWS CONSUMPTION**: Individuals often increase their news consumption after retirement, perceiving the world as more crisis-ridden than before, not because the world has significantly changed, but due to their increased exposure to sensationalized media.

PART III

PATHS FOR MANAGING FINANCES IN RETIREMENT

CHAPTER 14

EXPLORING THREE COMMON PATHS

In an earlier section of this book, I introduced the concept of *Retirement Zones*, each representing a distinct phase of the retirement journey. We observed that individuals naturally progress through these zones, each requiring different strategies. Through my experience working with people, I've noticed a common realization as retirement nears—the necessity to reevaluate their financial approach concerning savings and investments. As individuals approach retirement, they often contemplate one of three common paths for allocating their retirement funds. Today, I encourage you to explore these paths and then introduce an innovative alternative. Let's now delve into your options: three conventional approaches and one intriguing but less known path. When evaluating these strategies, consider how they aim to navigate the retirement pitfalls we've recently discussed. Do they effectively tackle them or fall short? Identify what is effective and what isn't. It is notable that many of these strategies only address certain risks and pitfalls.

PATH 1: PLAYING IT SAFE: "KEEPING IT IN THE BANK"

As individuals approach retirement, it›s common to have a specific monetary goal in mind for their 401K or savings. They envision reaching this target, cashing it in, and then investing the funds in low-risk options like money markets or CDs. I call this option *keeping it in the bank*. The idea is to live off the interest, protecting the principal and enjoying a blissful life. This strategy is like being at the summit of a mountain, providing a sense of security but hesitating to begin the descent. Similar to a climber, there's a danger of slowly exhausting your resources and failing to successfully descend. Although market fluctuations won't affect the nominal value of your money and you'll feel "safe," your money won't be experiencing significant growth, making it challenging to maintain your desired lifestyle. Unless you have substantial wealth, relying solely on interest earnings may not be sufficient.

Furthermore, tapping into your principal will diminish your financial resources over time. While this option eliminates risk for the money you plan to use in the near future, it hinders your long-term growth potential by not taking the necessary level of risk.

Advantages:

Placing all your funds in a bank account can indeed shield you from market downturns, eliminating risks. It effectively sidesteps the *Luck Factor* gamble of investments underperforming as you near retirement and during your initial retirement years.

Disadvantages:

However, this method lacks protection against *Inflation* and *Longevity Risks* in retirement. The income generated may struggle to keep up with inflation due to limited growth of the underlying assets. Over time, inflationary pressures might require dipping into both principal and interest, eroding savings and exposing individuals to the threat of outliving their financial resources.

PATH 2: GUARANTEED INCOME ANNUITY

Prospective retirees often contemplate investing their savings in guaranteed income annuities to secure a steady income during retirement. However, it's crucial to assess the trade-offs involved. While these annuities provide income stability, they necessitate relinquishing control over your wealth. They may not offer adequate income protection for your spouse and often lack adjustments for inflation, leaving you exposed in the long term. Despite potential advantages in specific scenarios, income annuities have garnered a negative reputation due to instances of being sold by insurance agents without prioritizing customers' best interests. While these annuities may seem attractive for income reliability, they come with notable constraints and may not effectively mitigate inflation risks or adequately safeguard your spouse. In my experience, while these can be suitable for certain individuals, it's uncommon for them to constitute the majority of one's savings.[2]

Advantages:

Investing in guaranteed income annuities provides a stable income source throughout retirement, offering

---

2 *Fixed Annuities are long term insurance contacts and there is a surrender charge imposed generally during the first 5 to 7 years that you own the annuity contract. Withdrawals prior to age 59-1/2 may result in a 10% IRS tax penalty, in addition to any ordinary income tax. Any guarantees of the annuity are backed by the financial strength of the underlying insurance company. Indexed annuities are insurance contracts that, depending on the contract, may offer a guaranteed annual interest rate and some participation growth, if any, of a stock market index. Such contracts have substantial variation in terms, costs of guarantees and features and may cap participation or returns in significant ways. Any guarantees offered are backed by the financial strength of the insurance company. Surrender charges apply if not held to the end of the term. Withdrawals are taxed as ordinary income and, if taken prior to 59 ½, a 10% federal tax penalty. Investors are cautioned to carefully review an indexed annuity for its features, costs, risks, and how the variables are calculated.

reassurance to those seeking to minimize financial uncertainties in later life. These financial tools offer peace of mind by ensuring a stable income regardless of market shifts, providing a lifelong guarantee.

Disadvantages:

One limitation is their failure to address inflation risk, as the income remains fixed over time. Additionally, they do not mitigate the longevity risk for a spouse, typically covering only the annuity holder's life. While a spouse can be added, the income would decrease accordingly due to the insurance company supporting two lives.

PATH 3: STICKING WITH WHAT HAS WORKED UP UNTIL THIS POINT: INVESTING ALL OF IT

Investing all your savings as you did before retiring is a common approach in retirement. It's tempting to believe that since it worked previously, it will work now. This method allows your wealth to potentially increase, and you can withdraw funds sustainably (usually 4-6%) throughout your life. However, if you encounter poor investment returns, particularly in the years leading up to retirement or early in retirement, this strategy may become troublesome, potentially depleting your funds. It's akin to rushing down a mountain before an approaching storm. Luck may be on your side, but it may not. Relying on luck or chance is unwise when it concerns your retirement. This method jeopardizes both your finances and your retirement.

Advantages:

This strategy offers a promising opportunity to generate a lifelong income that adjusts with inflation. In favorable circumstances, you may even expand your portfolio while receiving income, which is an appealing aspect. It helps mitigate risks including inflation, longevity, and common retirement pitfalls.

Disadvantages:

If conditions are unfavorable nearing retirement or in the initial decade from events such as a stock market crash or a bad recession, this method can swiftly erode retirement savings, necessitating a reduction in income. It may also be anxiety-inducing to nervously monitor the stock market, fearing that the next downturn could jeopardize your retirement.

SUMMARY OF KEY POINTS

- **KEEPING YOUR MONEY IN THE BANK:** This traditional method involves investing retirement savings in low-risk options such as money markets or CDs to live off the interest. While it provides a sense of security, it limits financial growth and long-term income sustainability.

- **GUARANTEED INCOME ANNUITY**: Offers income stability during retirement but at the cost of losing control over one's wealth. Despite the allure of predictable payments, annuities may not adequately protect against inflation or provide for a spouse.
- **INVESTING ALL YOUR SAVINGS**: Continuing to invest aggressively as before retirement can lead to growth, but it also poses significant risks, especially with poor market returns early in retirement, potentially depleting funds prematurely.

The common paths to retirement often overlook many retirement traps, leaving significant blind spots unaddressed. Is there a more effective approach we could consider?

CHAPTER 15

A BETTER PATH FORWARD: TIME SEGMENTATION

Having explored the traditional paths and identified the pitfalls each carries, it's clear that finding a balanced retirement strategy is no simple feat. The complexities of managing investments, navigating market volatility, and ensuring a steady income stream in retirement necessitates a nuanced approach. As we transition from these conventional paths, the next section will introduce a strategy that not only mitigates the risks associated with these traditional methods but also aligns with the goal of achieving a prosperous and worry-free retirement. This innovative approach promises to redefine retirement planning, offering a beacon of hope for those seeking a reliable income in their golden years.

TIME SEGMENTATION

Time Segmentation is a method my clients learn and implement, and I must confess it is my favorite preferred approach. Despite being widely accepted within the niche realm of advisors that specialize in distribution planning, this method remains somewhat obscure outside of those in retirement planning circles. It presents a sophisticated strategy for retirement income, and I see its potential as quite significant. I am a firm believer in its effectiveness in generating reliable retirement income. This strategy combines different techniques we've covered in the *Three Common Paths* section, harnessing their strengths while effectively addressing their weaknesses. Known as the *Time-Segmented Strategy*, I consider it the optimal route to establish a secure retirement income.

The essence of the *Time-Segmented Strategy* lies in crafting distinct investment plans for different phases, or time segments, of retirement. Early stages involve conservative and secure investments to help ensure a smooth transition from the most vulnerable phase. Looking ahead perhaps 15 years or more, a progressively aggressive investment strategy is embraced, offering growth opportunities without undue concern over market fluctuations affecting your finances in the near term.

Developing a well-structured *Time-Segmented Strategy* demands a blend of art and science. While I recommend professional guidance, I offer initial calculations to aid your comprehension and kickstart your planning journey, should you opt to proceed on your own. In the following segment, I will present an in-depth explanation of the functionality of *Time Segmentation*.

SUMMARY OF KEY POINTS

- **THE TIME-SEGMENTED STRATEGY**: An innovative approach integrating the strengths of other methods while avoiding their weaknesses, promising a balanced retirement. It involves crafting investment plans for different retirement phases, ensuring income reliability and growth opportunities.
- **IMPLEMENTATION OF TIME SEGMENTATION**: Involves strategic planning with both conservative and aggressive investments tailored for various retirement stages. A professional consultation is recommended to craft a tailored *Time-Segmented Strategy* for optimized retirement income.

CHAPTER 16

HOW TIME SEGMENTATION WORKS IN PRACTICE

Allow me to provide a more comprehensive explanation of how time segmentation works and can potentially benefit you.

In a hypothetical application of this strategy, your retirement funds are divided into six distinct time segments, each with a duration of five years. Within each segment, you will allocate a distinct level of money invested at a desired level of risk, ranging from conservative to aggressive, covering the entire spectrum of risk. It is important to note that your personal plan will likely differ from this hypothetical example in its details; however, the underlying principles illustrated in this example remain valid.

ESSENTIAL COMPONENTS OF THE STRATEGY.

- **SEGMENT 1:** The money you will need in the first five years of retirement is allocated to conservative financial products. These products provide an immediate source of income and serve as a safety net while you transition from the peak of your financial journey. In the event of a financial downturn, *Segment #1* acts as a strong safety line, firmly anchored to the mountain to help provide more confidence.

  On average, most people allocate around 20% of their available funds to this segment. It may come as a surprise that such a significant portion of your money is utilized within the first five years. However, this is due to the limited time when these funds are needed and thus the limited time available to grow them.

  With a solid footing in *Segment #1*, you will weather the first five years of retirement, effortlessly advancing towards your next milestone—*Segment #2* the next five years.

- **SEGMENT 2**: Your next checkpoint, the second segment, involves the funds you will need for years 6-10. These funds are also placed into conservative investments. But since you will be utilizing this money in five years, it is possible to invest it in five year investment options, offering the potential for higher returns than what was likely in *Segment #1* due to the longer lock-in period. Typically, around 20% of the available funds are allocated to this segment. Here we must avoid taking excessive risks and we do not expect exceptionally high returns. Once the funds are invested in this segment, we simply let them grow in a low-risk manner. There is little need for active management in *Segment #2* until year six commences. At the start of year six, the investments will then be liquidated and moved back to the same strategy used in *Segment #1*. Now, the funds will be utilized for current income, so the investment allocation is adjusted to options that prioritize security, safety, and consistent income. This strategy is straightforward and logical. As we progress through the segments, the funds gradually shift to the lower risk segment intended for generating income.

By completing this segment as well as the first one, you have successfully planned for your first 10 years of retirement. Congratulations on navigating the *Danger Zone*. Protecting the initial 10 years at the beginning of your plan now allows you to take slightly more risks with the subsequent segments.

- **SEGMENT 3:** The funds needed for years 11-15, also referred to as the third segment, should be directed towards investments carrying low to moderate risk. It's typical to allocate about 15% of your available capital to this segment. Despite having a 10-year investment horizon, prudence remains key. While the allure of the stock market is strong, given its historical performance over most ten-year spans, it's crucial to remember that it might not always meet expectations, potentially leading to losses or negligible returns.

  I call this the *Goldilocks* segment because it requires a carefully balanced investment approach—neither too conservative nor too risky. The goal here is to find a financial strategy or product that embodies moderate risk.

  Upon entering year 11, you should transition this segment to mirror the strategies used in *Segment #1*, which prioritizes low risk and reliable income. At this point, its role shifts towards generating immediate income, necessitating a shift to safer investment vehicles that help ensure stability, security, and steady income.

- **SEGMENT 4:** This segment refers to the money allocated for years 16-20 of your retirement. It compromises approximately 15% of your savings. *Segments #1, #2, and #3* have already covered the first 15 years.

Now that you have a 15-year window to let this money grow, it's the perfect opportunity to consider more aggressive investments. The longer time frame reduces the variability in long-term returns, providing a solid foundation for a more aggressive investment strategy. Aim for a target return that is indicative of a more aggressive investment portfolio. It's important to note that the average return is crucial here, rather than the order of returns.

Maintenance of *Segment #4* and beyond requires a key practice known as *Harvesting*. This entails monitoring the progress of the money in each segment and adjusting its investments as it approaches its target end value. The target value represents the amount necessary to fund the following five years when it will be needed. At this stage, it's advisable to transition from an aggressive strategy to a conservative one. Unnecessary risks should be avoided to help ensure that your account remains stable. Since average returns vary greatly from year to year, it's crucial to prevent wild swings and potential declines just when you need those funds. It's important to note that the purpose of a *Time Segmented Plan* is not to exceed your established plan, but rather to help ensure its successful execution. Rest assured that a significant portion of your money will still be invested, as you won't anticipate needing it for some time.

- **SEGMENT 5:** This segment represents the funds allocated for years 21-25, comprising around 10% of your initial resources. With a timeframe of 20 years, this segment allows ample opportunity for growth, which is why it starts with a smaller amount. A more aggressive investment strategy is recommended here, considering the extended duration and potential for higher returns. It is critical to emphasize the importance of *Harvesting* in this segment.
- **SEGMENT 6:** This segment follows the same overarching strategy as *Segment #5*, with a focus on growth. The allocated funds will be utilized during the years 26-30, making the *Harvesting* phase crucial in this period.
- **THE WEALTH BUILDING SEGMENT:** This is designated for funds to be utilized in years 31 and beyond. This portion comprises around 10% of your initial resources. The objective here is to cultivate this account with a view to recouping the original investment. It starts with modest amounts and adopts an aggressive investment approach. This strategy not only allows you to continue building your wealth, but also enables you to concurrently make use of your other funds. You may question the purpose of amassing additional wealth to leave behind for your children. However, I would argue that this is not solely for their benefit, but for

yours, as well. After all, your birth certificate lacks an expiration date, so it is unknown how long you will be alive. Moreover, unforeseen circumstances may arise later in life necessitating access to these funds. Additionally, you may outlive your original plan as advancements in medical science and technology continue to extend human lifespans. Therefore, it is critical to ensure that you possess the financial means to embrace life to the fullest rather than merely existing. This account is not subject to regular *Harvesting*; instead, we allow it to mature over the long term as far as your imagination can conceive.

TIPS FOR SETTING UP SEGMENTS:

Organize Your Accounts

Consider treating each segment as a separate account, complete with its own account number. This approach will greatly enhance organizational efficiency. In some cases, multiple accounts may flow into a single segment. To keep track of this, create a spreadsheet that includes each segment, its target rate of return, the allocated accounts, and the desired end value. This practice proves helpful during review sessions. Professionals often have specialized tools to assist with segment organization, but if you're working independently, you'll need to devise your own system.

LOGISTICS: HOW TO PAY YOURSELF FROM YOUR INVESTMENTS

You have the flexibility to set up the frequency of payouts according to your preference. While certain aspects such as pensions and Social Security are usually arranged for you, you have control over how you withdraw funds from your investments. Whether it's monthly, weekly, or quarterly, it's your money and you get to decide.

It's intriguing how people are often interested in the nitty-gritty of structuring their income rather than just the high-level investing concepts. Specifically, they want to know how to seamlessly transfer funds from their retirement resources to their bank accounts. Here's a model that you may find useful:

Most likely, you already have a primary checking account, which will serve as your income account. This is where all your deposits will go. To begin, set up your income floor resources such as Social Security and any pensions to be directly deposited into this account on a predetermined day each month, quarter, or other interval. Monthly is a popular choice because it aligns with what you may have been accustomed to during your working years. It's advisable to arrange for tax withholding from each of these income streams so that the taxes are withheld on your behalf and paid directly to the IRS. This eliminates the need for you to manage it separately. For estimates on tax withholding, consult a tax advisor or your financial advisor.

Next, arrange for the income from your investment accounts to be directly deposited into your income account on a set schedule, whether it's monthly, quarterly, or yearly. Once again, monthly is often preferred. If the account you're using for this purpose is a 401K, Traditional IRA, or any other retirement account that defers taxes, I recommend withholding taxes from this income stream, as well. By doing so, taxes are automatically withheld, sparing you the hassle of dealing with quarterly tax payments.

By following these steps, you'll establish a steady and predictable cash flow. It will resemble the structure to which you were accustomed during your working years. Remember, you can customize the timing to suit your needs to a certain extent.

The beauty of this setup is that most retirement account providers or investment companies offer complimentary services such as linking your bank account, setting up monthly distributions, and tax withholding. This adds value and convenience because once the setup is complete, you only need to make occasional adjustments as your circumstances evolve or if you change bank accounts.

ADVANCED TECHNIQUES:

Income Floor

To ensure a comprehensive understanding of your income sources beyond personal savings, it is crucial to acknowledge additional streams such as social security and pensions. Take into account any guaranteed income and determine precise amounts and start dates by carefully reviewing statements or reaching out to the provider. It is equally important to assess whether these amounts are inflation protected and offer benefits to your beneficiaries.

Harvesting

As mentioned earlier, *Harvesting* plays a critical role in monitoring your progress. It is a method of effectively managing the risk associated with the sequence of returns. By safeguarding the funds you will be utilizing in the near future from potential downturns, you consistently search for opportunities to protect them once they have achieved their intended purpose or have reached a point where they can fulfill their ultimate goal with minimal risk. This necessitates monitoring each segment and understanding how the account is progressing toward its objective. From there, it becomes a judgment call on how to manage the investments within each segment. Should you continue taking risks, or is it possible to achieve your goals without them?

Segment Zero

Let's dive into *Segment Zero*—the holding period. Imagine you want to retire exactly three years from today. When should you start planning? *Segment Zero* allows you to set up or schedule your retirement date by employing an advanced strategy. By allocating the money that will kickstart your plan into *Segment Zero*, you safeguard yourself from the *Order of Returns Risk* as you approach retirement. This means you set aside the exact amount of money you'll need in the year of your retirement, allowing it to grow in a conservative investment that matures precisely when you need it.

This approach is effective because you have a clear understanding of the funds required for the initial five years of your retirement. Although it may be a few years away, you can set it aside today, building it up over time or, at the very least, protecting it. You may argue that you prefer to keep the money invested. However, as you near retirement, the potential downside outweighs the limited upside of staying invested. A good year in the stock market is unlikely to significantly enhance your plan, while a particularly bad year could potentially delay your retirement for several years.

To customize your plan according to important life events such as qualifying for social security or starting a pension, you have the flexibility to add or remove segments. I advise you align these segments with significant milestones in your financial journey. For instance, if you plan to start receiving Social Security at age 62 but retire at age 60, consider making your first segment only two years long. This way, you can initiate a new segment that incorporates your social security benefits, allowing for a reduced reliance on investment funds.

Which Accounts To Use First

When deciding which accounts to prioritize, it's important to weigh the advantages and disadvantages of utilizing assets within specific segments. A crucial factor to consider is the tax implications, as certain accounts may be subject to higher taxation than others. A well-crafted plan should take into account these tax considerations, as well as any unique characteristics of specific accounts, such as an inherited IRA. These may include 401Ks, IRAs, non-IRA accounts, and riskier investments like stock options. By carefully assessing these factors, you can make informed decisions that optimize your financial strategy.

To learn more, here is an additional resource:

CHAPTER 17

10 ADVANTAGES OF TIME SEGMENTATION

ADVANTAGE 1: PRECISION OF YOUR RETIREMENT DATE SCHEDULING

Choose to retire on your own terms, at your desired time. By creating a time-segmented plan, you can schedule your retirement according to your preferences. This is achieved through ensuring that your financial needs in the first decade of retirement are secure. There's no longer any guesswork about your income or its sources during the initial ten years of your retirement, so you can put a date on the calendar and know it's your target.

Accomplishing this requires a different mindset than what you may be used to. While it might be appealing to maintain all your funds in high-risk investments if that has been your strategy so far, doing this exposes you to the uncertainties of short-term stock market performance. Be assured that you won't forgo potential investment gains, as a substantial portion of your funds will still benefit from positive stock market performance.

ADVANTAGE 2: RISK MANAGEMENT

Risk in investing is often misunderstood, yet it plays a crucial role in financial planning. When harnessed effectively, risk can be a potent tool in your investment strategy. In the realm of investments, risk doesn't equate to the permanent loss of funds, but rather reflects the fluctuation of your assets relative to the broader market—a concept encapsulated by volatility. Greater fluctuations translate to higher volatility and increased risk. The level of risk inherent in an investment influences its expected return—higher risks are typically associated with higher potential returns, while lower risks are linked to reduced expected returns.

Time Segmentation provides a structured approach to enhance risk management effectiveness. By allocating your investments across different time segments, you can effectively manage the risks associated with each segment. It's akin to putting fire in an oven—harnessing the power of fire by using it wisely. Embrace risk intelligently instead of avoiding it altogether. Although risky investments may be uncertain in the short run, historical data proves that they deliver consistent returns over extended periods. Therefore, consider investing in riskier assets for long-term objectives, while adopting a more cautious strategy for short-term necessities. This balanced approach offers assurance that you are leveraging risk effectively by safeguarding your immediate needs with safer investments, while also positioning yourself for growth through riskier investments for the future.

ADVANTAGE 3: FIGHTING INFLATION

Empower yourself with a regular *Cost of Living Adjustment (COLA)* to account for increasing expenses in retirement. Maintaining income to match rising costs is vital, and you can customize this adjustment to fit your needs. While I personally suggest a 2% or 3% COLA, feel free to tailor it to your unique requirements.

Time Segmentation allows you to factor in an anticipated inflation rate into your financial plan. This involves allocating funds in a way such that if growth targets are achieved, you will generate income in line with your inflation projections.

As previously mentioned, *Inflation* stands out as one of the *Retirement Traps* that numerous distribution strategies overlook.

ADVANTAGE 4: MORE RATIONAL DECISIONS/ LESS EMOTIONAL DECISIONS

By minimizing the impact of emotions, you will enhance your happiness and confidence. This assurance is rooted in securing the money needed for the initial phase of your retirement, usually covering the first 10 years as per your plan. With this understanding, you'll have the strength to navigate stock market fluctuations with resilience.

This safety net offers relief to your limbic system, the fight-or-flight center of your brain. When triggered, this part may prompt hasty decisions driven by emotions such as fear. The strategy shields you from reacting impulsively in high-stakes financial situations or during everyday activities. It becomes evident that the day-to-day market changes and economic fluctuations have minimal impact on your current strategy, as your long-term plan has already considered the expected volatility from more risky investments.

ADVANTAGE #5 MAINTAINING A FINANCIAL RESERVE

A *Time Segmented Plan* offers the opportunity to establish a financial reserve by establishing the *Wealth Building Segment*, which is critical for various reasons. While spending all your hard-earned savings may be tempting, it's vital to prioritize ongoing wealth accumulation in retirement. Aiming to finish with the same amount you began with, such as turning $1,000,000 from an initial investment of $1,000,000, serves as a strong starting goal. This not only establishes a financial safety net for unforeseen expenses but also guards against outliving your plan (which we wish for you!). This preserved capital can cover unforeseen costs, ensuring your income plan remains intact. Even if you don't retain your original principal, this financial reserve positions you in a stronger financial stance.

ADVANTAGE 6: CLARITY OF YOUR INCOME SOURCES

Knowledge is truly power, and a *Time Segmentation* plan offers a profound insight into your income and its sources. Many individuals on the final stretch to retirement remain uncertain about their expected income sources in retirement. Understanding the origins of your income will provide reassurance and clarity, enabling you to forecast your income streams and make necessary adjustments in response to life changes. This knowledge also allows for strategic planning, such as optimizing tax planning by adjusting the distribution of income from different sources to achieve the most advantageous taxable levels. Moreover, gaining clarity on potential scenarios, such as the impact of a spouse's passing on income streams, offers a proactive approach over a passive "wait and see" mindset.

ADVANTAGE 7: WRITTEN PLANS ARE BETTER

A written plan holds unique power, and *Time Segmented* plans are written, being tangible, actionable, and as a reference guide to clarify questions or understand the course of action. I think those with written retirement plans tend to feel more confident, having thoroughly explored their options. However, a plan need not be lengthy or filled with unnecessary details. Personally, I prefer a concise 10-15-page report that is accurate, tailored, relevant, and practical. What matters is its utility, providing something truly beneficial. I appreciate tangible plans intentionally crafted on paper. There's satisfaction in making the intangible tangible. Other distribution strategies may generate written plans, but I have frequently observed them to be either too simplistic or excessively complex, both of which diminish their efficacy as planning tools.

ADVANTAGE 8: CUSTOMIZED AND UNIQUE TO YOU

Time Segmentation allows you to create a personalized plan that caters to your unique needs. By utilizing a time segmented approach, you can customize different segments according to your financial requirements. For instance, if you plan to retire at 62 and anticipate higher expenses for health insurance premiums until age 65 when Medicare begins, you can allocate more resources during the first segment to cover those costs, gradually reducing them afterward. Alternatively, if you prioritize early travel experiences, you can adjust your financial plan to accommodate lower expenses in later stages of life.

ADVANTAGE 9: "RELIABILITY OF INCOME: YOUR NEW ROI METRIC

Time Segmentation shifts your focus from *Return on Investment (ROI)* to a new metric, the *Reliability of Income (ROI).*

During the accumulation phase, your primary concern is *Return on Investment.* However, as you transition to the distribution phase, your focus changes to the crucial aspect of *Reliability of Income.* In essence, it signifies a shift from accumulation to distribution. Although this change may appear minor, it represents a significant paradigm shift that can profoundly impact the success of your retirement. There are several compelling reasons why this shift holds such importance.

First and foremost, when you rely on your investments for retirement income, you become more vulnerable to market fluctuations. As you near retirement, your ability to recover from a market setback diminishes. If you're retired and dependent on your portfolio for income, a substantial loss can be devastating. Exclusively emphasizing *Return on Investment* may tempt you to assume excessive risks.

Moreover, conventional retirement guidance often fails to acknowledge that people are leading longer, healthier lives. As a result, your retirement funds may need to support you for 30+ years or more. It's critical to consider the *Longevity Risk* that led to a *Retirement Trap* previously. Placing excessive focus on *Return on Investment* may result in a narrow perspective of your investments. This focus on short-term market conditions may divert attention from the crucial long-term growth required to sustain income reliability over the years ahead. Consider the potential outcomes in 30 years rather than being solely fixated on current circumstances.

ADVANTAGE 10: FLEXIBILITY

One of the key strengths of a *Time Segmented* plan lies in its ability to adapt to life's changes. Whether it's health issues, relocating to a new home, or other transitions, recognizing the trade-offs is crucial. You have the flexibility to prioritize higher income early on or later, or even to rejoin the workforce. Unexpected opportunities may emerge, underscoring the significance of stability and adaptability in *Time Segmentation* compared to other retirement approaches that confine you to specific financial products or strategies. *Time Segmentation* enables adjustments on a segment-by-segment basis, providing flexibility within each period. This is mainly because with *Time Segmentation*, we operate in manageable time increments such as five-year segments without needing to falsely believe in pinpoint accuracy to map out your life to the cent and assume everything will unfold exactly as planned.

PART IV

RETIREMENT READINESS

CHAPTER 18

MORTGAGES IN RETIREMENT

When it comes to mortgages and retirement, a simplistic approach may advise you to pay it off before you retire. However, it's essential to note that this isn't a one-size-fits-all scenario. Yes, entering retirement mortgage-free is an admirable goal, yet for many, carrying a mortgage into retirement is a reality. If you find yourself in this situation, don't panic.

As retirement looms and your mortgage remains, it's time to shift focus. Instead of fixating on eliminating your mortgage entirely, prioritize effective cash flow management. Aim to maintain manageable mortgage payments. Remember, in retirement, avoid compromising your lifestyle solely to clear your mortgage debt.

REFINANCING

Avoid the temptation of choosing a 15-year mortgage close to retirement to swiftly pay off your mortgage. The increased monthly payments may strain your finances. Instead, be vigilant for refinancing opportunities that could lower your monthly expenses. When considering refinancing, keep the following factors in mind:

- After retirement, verifying your income may become more challenging, given that it will likely come from social security, pensions, and investments. Refinancing before retiring may be prudent.
- Exercise caution if your current mortgage rate is already competitive. The fees involved in refinancing may not be worth it.

TO PAY OFF OR NOT TO PAY OFF BEFORE RETIREMENT

As for the debate of whether to pay off your mortgage before retirement, consider your future plans. If you're likely to move, paying off your mortgage might not be the best choice. If settling down for a long time in your current home is part of your plan, prioritizing mortgage payments could be a smarter move.

THE TAX IMPLICATIONS OF KEEPING A MORTGAGE

Lastly, when it comes to taxes, don't keep a mortgage only for the interest deduction. The financial formula may not work in your favor. The IRS may reduce your taxes for every dollar you pay in interest, but remember, the majority of your payment still goes to the bank as interest. Plus, under current tax rules, everyone is entitled to a hefty standard deduction. Your mortgage interest may not exceed this standard deduction, making the interest deduction strategy potentially moot.

SUMMARY OF KEY POINTS

- When approaching retirement with a mortgage, the focus should be on managing cash flow and ensuring manageable monthly payments rather than trying to entirely pay off the mortgage. Avoid taking 15-year mortgages at retirement, as they could put a strain on your finances.
- Refinancing opportunities should be explored for potentially lowering monthly payments. However, post-retirement income validation could be challenging, your existing mortgage rate may already be competitive and opting for a 30-year loan mostly has tax-deductible interest in the early payments.

- The decision to pay off your mortgage before retirement depends on your future plans. If you're planning to move, it may not be beneficial, but if you're settling in your current home for a long time, it could be a smart move. Do not retain a mortgage solely for the interest deduction, as it may not be financially advantageous, especially considering the current tax rules and standard deductions.

CHAPTER 19

REVERSE MORTGAGE OVERVIEW

A *Reverse Mortgage* is a loan that allows homeowners to access the equity in their homes while still living in them without the need for repayment until they move out or pass away. In 1988, President Ronald Reagan signed the *Reverse Mortgage* bill into law, granting the *U.S. Department of Housing and Urban Development (HUD)* the authority to insure *Reverse Mortgages* through the *Federal Housing Administration (FHA)*. This marked a significant step toward integrating reverse mortgages into the realm of personal finance. This type of loan enables homeowners to remain in their homes while benefiting from the accumulated equity. Over the years, it has undergone refinements and improvements.

ELIGIBILITY REQUIRMENTS

Requirements for obtaining a *Reverse Mortgage* include being 62 years or older and typically having at least 50% equity in your home.

ADVANTAGES OF A REVERSE MORTGAGE

The funds are usually tax-free, you don't have to repay the loan until you no longer live in your home, and you retain ownership of your home. Additionally, it generally does not impact your Social Security or Medicare benefits, and you have the flexibility to use the proceeds for any purpose. You can receive the funds in a lump sum, as periodic payments, or as a line of credit.

DOWNSIDES OF A REVERSE MORTGAGE

A *Reverse Mortgage* reduces your home equity, and interest on the loan balance accrues, diminishing your equity further. You also lose the satisfaction of owning your home outright, and repayment of the loan includes accrued interest. As a homeowner with a *Reverse Mortgage*, you are still responsible for paying property taxes and insurance, maintaining the property, and using it as your primary residence for at least half of the year.

INDUSTRY PERSPECTIVES AND CRITICAL VIEWS

It's evident that *Reverse Mortgages* elicit a wide range of responses within the financial planning industry. Some experts view them as a viable option, while others vehemently oppose them. In forming my stance on the matter, I have strived to amass diverse perspectives and data before drawing conclusions.

Notably, the key criticism of *Reverse Mortgages* lies within the personal values associated with homeownership and the independence it signifies. Critics also highlight the higher fees, interest rates, and default rates as compared to traditional mortgages—with default and foreclosure rates reportedly as high as 18%, versus about 3% for standard mortgages.

However, it's essential to consider that reverse mortgages are often a recourse for individuals already in financial straits—not a cause of their predicament. The elevated interest rates reflect an increased risk of default, and the additional fees are simply the cost of doing business.

Therefore, in my opinion, the arguments against *Reverse Mortgages* are somewhat superficial and largely driven by personal values surrounding homeownership rather than purely quantitative financial assessments.

MY OBSERVATIONS ON REVERSE MORTGAGES

In my experience, those who typically resort to a *Reverse Mortgage* tend to be older individuals, usually in their 80s, who find themselves in a precarious financial situation. They possess significant home equity but lack other substantial resources. Thus, they utilize a *Reverse Mortgage* as a means to access those funds. This demographic aligns with my expectations of the average *Reverse Mortgage* user, and it likely contributes to the higher default and interest rates associated with *Reverse Mortgages* compared to traditional ones. These individuals are already confronting financial hardship—not a result of adopting a *Reverse Mortgage*, but a precursor to it.

The issue arises from the fact that even with a *Reverse Mortgage*, there are still obligations to pay real estate taxes, insurance, and maintain the property. Failure to fulfill these responsibilities, particularly regarding taxes and insurance, can result in the bank foreclosing on the loan, which may necessitate selling your house to settle the loan balance. However, when you consider it, this situation isn't significantly different from owning your house outright. Non-payment of taxes can lead to foreclosure by the taxing authority.

On the opposing side of the argument, there are those who believe that *Reverse Mortgages* can be advantageous. They contend that such financial arrangements can serve as a viable solution for individuals with limited retirement funds but substantial home equity. By utilizing a *Reverse*

Mortgage, homeowners can access their equity, continue residing in their house, and are not required to repay the loan until they no longer occupy the property.

If you anticipate being unable to meet the financial obligations of taxes and insurance, it may not be a prudent choice. Avoid unnecessary complications and seek a more suitable living arrangement. Consider utilizing the equity in your current home to partially or fully fund your new house. Keep an open mind regarding this product and evaluate its suitability only if necessary. While paying off your mortgage is undoubtedly a commendable goal, it should not be the sole focus. Other factors also hold significance. If you possess substantial home equity but lack liquid assets, a *Reverse Mortgage* could be an option worth considering. It is important to be aware that fees will be incurred, as there is no such thing as a free lunch. Additionally, the bank may impose a higher interest rate due to the increased market risk and reduced competition. Remember that there are still expenses that need to be covered.

Foreclosure on a *Reverse Mortgage* can occur due to several reasons. The most common cause is the failure to meet mandatory obligations such as paying property taxes, homeowners insurance, and costs for property maintenance. Borrowers must also live in the mortgaged property as their primary residence. If they relocate or are absent for an extended period, the lender may consider it a breach of contract and initiate foreclosure proceedings. Death of the borrower also triggers foreclosure unless the surviving spouse or heirs can settle the loan or sell the property to cover the loan balance. Lastly, if the property's value dips significantly, causing the loan balance to exceed the home's worth, foreclosure could ensue, although this is a less common scenario.

REVERSE MORTGAGES WITH MY CLIENTS

Reverse Mortgages can indeed be a vital tool for individuals finding themselves financially strapped beyond the age of 80. As average life expectancies extend into the lower to mid-90s, the availability of additional funds from such a mortgage can significantly ease the financial burden of those extra years.

In terms of my clientele, I have yet to encounter a client who has opted for a *Reverse Mortgage*. While several have contemplated the idea, none have chosen to move forward with it. This is likely due to the fact that most of my clients are financially stable. They either fully own their homes or have sufficient income to comfortably handle their mortgage payments. In our discussions, we position a *Reverse Mortgage* as a *Plan B*—a fallback option if unexpected financial needs arise. This perspective shifts the conversation around home equity and *Reverse Mortgages* from one of immediate need to one of strategic planning for future uncertainties. It's a way to unlock the value tied up in a home, should the need arise.

SUMMARY OF KEY POINTS

- *Reverse Mortgages* are a contentious topic in the financial planning industry, with debates often centered around the values of homeownership, higher fees, and increased default and foreclosure rates. However, Reverse Mortgages are often utilized by older individuals in dire financial circumstances who have substantial home equity but limited other resources.
- The major downside of Reverse Mortgages lies in the continuing obligations of the borrower to pay real estate taxes, insurance, and maintain the property. Failure to fulfill these duties can lead to foreclosure by the bank. However, Reverse Mortgages can also be seen as a viable solution for individuals with limited retirement funds but significant home equity, as they allow homeowners to tap into this equity without needing to leave their home.
- In terms of client experiences, while several have considered the idea of Reverse Mortgages, none have chosen to proceed, likely due to their financial stability. Reverse Mortgages are suggested as a *Plan B* to cater for unexpected financial needs, shifting the conversation from immediate necessity to strategic planning for future uncertainties.

CHAPTER 20

UNDERSTANDING REQUIRED MINIMUM DISTRIBUTIONS (RMDS)

THE BASICS OF RMDs

Required Minimum Distributions (RMDs) can initially appear complex, leading to confusion among retirees. However, the principle behind them is quite simple—these are the minimum amounts that you must withdraw from your retirement account annually starting from the age of 73. The IRS calculates this amount based on your life expectancy and account balance from the previous year. RMD is typically a percentage of this balance, often around 4% at age 73, but can vary due to several conditions.

AVOIDING THE 50% PENALTY

If you fail to withdraw your RMD by the end of the year, a significant 50% penalty may be incurred. This requirement to withdraw exists because the government has the right to tax a portion of your account as income, and the RMD mechanism guarantees the prompt distribution of these funds for taxation. Understanding and correctly managing RMDs can help avoid unwanted penalties and maximize your retirement savings.

THE "STILL WORKING" EXCEPTION

A potential exception to the RMD rule exists for those who choose to continue working past the age of 73 and decide to keep their money in their current 401(k). This exception, often referred to as the *Still Working Exception*, allows you to delay taking RMDs from your current employer's 401(k) as long as you're still actively employed, do not own more than 5% of the company, and are part of the company's 401(k) plan. Once you retire or leave the job, you would then be required to start taking RMDs, with the first distribution due by April 1st of the year following your retirement. This loophole could be beneficial to those planning on working into their later years and looking for ways to defer taxable income. However, it's crucial to note that this exception does not apply to IRAs or 401(k)s from previous employers.

SUMMARY OF KEY POINTS:

- *Required Minimum Distributions (RMDs)* are mandatory withdrawals from a retirement account that start once an individual reaches the age of 73. The amount to be withdrawn, determined by the IRS, is typically a percentage of the previous year's account balance and depends on the individual's age and life expectancy.
- Failing to withdraw the RMD by the end of the year can lead to a severe 50% penalty. This requirement exists because the government can tax a portion of the retirement account as income, and RMDs make sure these funds are distributed in a timely manner to facilitate taxation.
- Understanding and properly managing RMDs can help retirees avoid hefty penalties and make the most of their retirement savings, simplifying what may initially seem like a complex financial system into a clear-cut strategy.
- The *Still Working Exception* is a loophole that allows individuals who continue working past the age of 73 to delay their RMDs from their current employer's 401(k), given they're still employed, don't own more than 5% of the company, and are part of the company's 401(k) plan. This exception does not apply to IRAs or 401(k)s from former employers. However, you may have the option to consolidate those old accounts into your current 401K, thereby circumventing the requirement for RMDs.

CHAPTER 21

INTRODUCTION TO IRAS

Almost every retiree I know has at least one Individual Retirement Account (IRA) when they retire. These accounts commonly serve as a destination for the money they've saved in their 401K. Consequently, it is crucial to be well-versed in a few key aspects regarding these accounts.

There are two main types of Individual Retirement Accounts (IRAs): Traditional and Roth. Traditional IRAs are the more widely used option, where the funds are contributed on a pre-tax basis. This means that if you make a withdrawal, you will be required to pay taxes on the amount. On the other hand, Roth IRAs are funded with after-tax money, and any withdrawals you make from it are completely tax-free.

TRADITIONAL IRAs

Based on my experience, most retirement savers are familiar with *Traditional IRAs*. They often use them to consolidate various types of accounts, such as 401Ks, 401K, SEP, 457, TSP, or as a savings account for annual contributions.

Chances are, you'll also be utilizing an IRA during your retirement. These accounts are highly beneficial as they allow you to transfer funds from virtually any retirement plan into your own IRA. This provides you with the flexibility to withdraw money from employer-sponsored plans like 401Ks, SEP, 457, TSP, or 403B plans and transfer it to your personal account once you are no longer employed.

Here are some important points to consider about *Traditional IRAs* as you approach retirement:

Early withdrawals before age 59-1/2 are subject to a 10% penalty.

Withdrawals from a Traditional IRA are taxed at your regular income tax rate. You will receive a 1099-R tax form at the end of the year, which will show the amount withdrawn and the taxes withheld. If you paid too much in taxes, you will receive a refund. If you didn't pay enough, you will owe the IRS.

Once you reach a certain age, currently 73, you must start taking required minimum distributions (RMD) from your IRA. More information on RMD can be found in the prior section of this book.

Your IRA has a designated beneficiary. In the event of your death, the money in the account will go to the beneficiary. If your spouse is the beneficiary, the money can be transferred directly to their IRA. If the beneficiary is someone other than your spouse, they will receive the money in an inherited IRA and will be required to use it within a specific period, including taking required minimum distributions.

In an IRA, you can hold a wide range of investment products, including stocks, bonds, mutual funds, fixed annuities, equity indexed annuities, and variable annuities. Think of your IRA as a tax-advantaged account that holds various investments rather than an investment itself.

ROTH IRAs

Roth IRAs are less commonly utilized for people currently nearing retirement. While financial magazines often feature articles about them, they are not frequently employed in real-world practice for savers who are mid to late career. This may be due to the fact that they are funded with after-tax deposits, which may not be as appealing to individuals earning high incomes and seeking maximum tax benefits for their IRA contributions. Additionally, *Roth IRAs* are typically incompatible with many employer-sponsored plans.

In a *Roth IRA*, the money you contribute has already been taxed. The advantage is that this money can now grow tax-free, and when you make withdrawals, both the amount you initially deposited and any gains you have made are exempt from taxes. The prospect of tax-free withdrawals is what entices many people.

UNDERSTANDING ROTH CONVERSIONS

In recent years, Roth conversions have emerged as a hot topic in the realm of retirement planning. This heightened interest can be traced back to a pivotal legislative change that permitted the conversion of *Traditional IRAs* into *Roth IRAs*. The distinction between these two types of IRAs is fundamental to understanding the appeal of Roth conversions. *Traditional IRAs* are characterized by their pre-tax contributions, meaning that withdrawals are taxed. Conversely, *Roth IRAs* are funded with after-tax dollars, allowing for tax-free growth and withdrawals.

The process of converting a *Traditional IRA* into a *Roth IRA* involves paying taxes on the converted amount. For example, converting a $100,000 *Traditional IRA* balance would, assuming a 20% tax rate, result in a $20,000 tax bill. If the conversion tax is paid using funds from the IRA itself, this might trigger an additional 10% penalty for premature withdrawal if done prior to age 59-1/2, necessitating a larger withdrawal to cover both the tax and the penalty. Despite this upfront cost, the future benefit of tax-free withdrawals from a Roth IRA can be attractive.

However, it's critical to consider one's place in the retirement planning timeline before opting for a Roth conversion. While the tax-free advantages of a *Roth IRA* are more pronounced for those early in their retirement savings journey, individuals approaching retirement may find the conversion less beneficial. Consequently, a Roth conversion is not a one-size-fits-all solution, and its suitability varies based on individual financial circumstances and retirement planning stages.

> ***Disclosure:*** *Converting an employer plan account or Traditional IRA to a Roth IRA is a taxable event. Increased taxable income from the Roth IRA conversion may have several consequences including but not limited to, a need for additional tax withholding or estimated tax payments, the loss of certain tax deductions and credits, and higher taxes on Social Security benefits and higher Medicare premiums. Be sure to consult with a qualified tax advisor before making any decisions regarding your IRA.*

SUMMARY OF KEY POINTS

- IRAs are a popular choice for retirees to consolidate various types of retirement savings accounts, such as 401Ks, SEP, 457, or TSP. *Traditional IRAs*, funded with pre-tax money, and *Roth IRAs*, funded with after-tax money, offer different benefits and tax implications.
- The choice between *Traditional* and *Roth IRAs* hinges on the individual's tax situation and retirement goals. While *Traditional IRAs* require taxes to be paid during withdrawal, *Roth IRAs* allow for tax-free withdrawal. However, *Roth IRAs* demand taxes to be paid upfront at the time of contribution.

- Roth conversions have gained popularity in recent years, enabling individuals to convert their *Traditional IRA* to a *Roth IRA*. This process involves paying taxes on the current balance of the *Traditional IRA* but allows for tax-free growth and withdrawal in the future. This strategy, however, is generally more suited to individuals in the early stages of their savings journey.

CHAPTER 22

MOVING MONEY FROM EMPLOYER-SPONSORED PLANS

THE CASE FOR ROLLOVERS TO AN IRA

Why would someone choose to transfer money out of an employer-sponsored plan like a 401K? In my view, there are two key advantages of rolling your money into an IRA: control and flexibility. By doing so, you gain more control over your finances as the IRA becomes your personal account, eliminating the need to rely on your employer or their chosen plan sponsor. Additionally, an IRA provides you with greater flexibility by offering a wider range of investment options compared to most 401K plans. With an IRA, you have access to a diverse selection of investment products which can play a critical role in your retirement plan. While a 401K is designed to cater to a large number of people, an IRA can be tailored to suit the unique needs of an individual.

RETAINING FUNDS IN EMPLOYER-SPONSORED PLANS

However, there are advantages provided by employer-sponsored plans that should be taken into account. What would motivate someone to retain their funds in such a plan? Here are several compelling reasons to consider remaining:

- **ACCESS TO LOW-COST FUNDS**: If your employer plan is large and has a significant number of participants, the costs of the plan are spread out, resulting in lower expenses.
- **DIVERSE INVESTMENT OPTIONS**: Many retirement accounts now offer an expanding range of investment options. This means you have the flexibility to choose investments that align with your financial goals and risk tolerance, all within the convenience of your plan.
- **CREDITOR PROTECTION**: Another important advantage offered by most 401K plans is that these plans are generally protected from creditors under the *Employee Retirement Income Security Act (ERISA)*. This means that in the event of bankruptcy or lawsuits, your 401K assets are usually shielded from claims made by creditors. It's a valuable layer of protection that can help ensure your retirement

savings stay intact, even if you encounter financial difficulties. In contrast, IRA creditor protections vary widely and are largely determined by state laws, potentially making 401Ks a safer choice for those concerned about asset protection. Consult with a financial advisor or legal professional to understand the specifics of how these protections apply to your individual circumstances.

IN-SERVICE WITHDRAWALS

Some employer-sponsored plans offer the option of taking a distribution before retirement, known as *in-service withdrawals*. However, not all plans allow this.

RATIONALE BEHIND IN-SERVICE WITHDRAWALS

In-service withdrawals provide the opportunity to withdraw some or all of the funds from your plan while still working and roll them into a *Traditional IRA*. This allows you to proactively plan for your retirement by setting up specific investments that are not available in your 401K. If your plan does not offer in-service withdrawals, there are still ways to make your plan work, although it may not be as convenient or tailored to your specific needs as an individual IRA. Typically, in-service withdrawals are subject to certain age requirements, usually around 59-½.

Why would someone consider an *in-service withdrawal*? It provides the flexibility to customize your financial plan for retirement as you approach that stage of life. While employer-sponsored plans are generally designed to cater to a broad range of employees, as you near retirement, you may require different investment options that are not available within your employer's plan. An *in-service withdrawal* allows you to tailor your plan to meet your specific needs, whether it's accessing certain products or services or having more control over your investment choices.

Some individuals choose to take an *in-service withdrawal* for a portion of their funds to address the limitations of their 401(k) plan. This approach enables them to set up a retirement plan while still utilizing their employer-sponsored plan as their primary investment account. It is uncommon for retirees to keep their funds in an employer-sponsored plan, as they often seek closure and desire more control over their assets. One exception to this trend is government employees, who tend to remain loyal to their TSP plans.

Overall, *in-service withdrawals* provide an avenue for early planning and customization, empowering individuals to shape their retirement strategy according to their unique circumstances and goals.

SUMMARY OF KEY POINTS

- **IRA ROLLOVERS PROVIDE CONTROL AND FLEXIBILITY**: Transferring funds from employer-sponsored plans such as 401Ks to an IRA offer individuals greater control over their investments and a broader range of investment options, tailoring retirement plans to meet personal needs.
- **BENEFITS OF EMPLOYER-SPONSORED PLANS**: These plans may offer access to low-cost funds, a diverse range of investment options, and significant creditor protection under the *Employee Retirement Income Security Act (ERISA)*, making them a competitive option for safeguarding retirement savings.
- **CREDITOR PROTECTION VARIANCE**: While 401K plans offer robust creditor protection, IRA protections depend on state laws, meaning the level of protection against creditors can vary significantly from one state to another.
- **IN-SERVICE WITHDRAWALS FOR EARLY PLANNING**: In-service withdrawals from employer-sponsored plans allow for early rollovers into *Traditional IRAs*, providing an opportunity to customize investment strategies prior to retirement, especially when specific plan limitations are encountered.

- **STRATEGIC UTILIZATION OF EMPLOYER PLANS AND IRAs**: Individuals can optimize their retirement planning by leveraging both employer-sponsored plans and IRAs, using *in-service withdrawals* when necessary to overcome the limitations of 401(k) plans and prepare more personalized retirement strategies.

CHAPTER 23

DECIDING WHEN TO TAKE SOCIAL SECURITY

Deciding when to start receiving social security benefits can be a challenging decision. It's difficult to determine the right choice amidst conflicting advice. Many online sources suggest waiting until age 70 to maximize payments, while friends and family who are already receiving benefits will have their own opinions on when the best time to start is. So what is the right approach?

While the online proponents have a point—waiting until age 70 can indeed result in higher benefits—this perspective oversimplifies the matter. In my experience, waiting until age 70 is not always the optimal time to start receiving social security benefits.

In many cases, it is actually more advantageous to start receiving benefits in the year of retirement. If you retire at 62, that may be the appropriate time to begin. If you retire at age 65, then that may become the suitable time. Delaying the receipt of social security benefits means bridging the gap by relying on other sources of income to cover living expenses, depleting resources that could have otherwise grown over time. By pulling money from the later stages of your financial plan and redirecting it to the early years where it cannot accumulate, you may be compromising your overall financial strategy. That's why, in most instances, it is preferable to start receiving benefits in the year of retirement.

While it may seem logical to wait until age 70 when viewed in isolation, it is crucial to consider all your combined resources and their long-term implications. Taking into account the broader context, it becomes evident that starting social security benefits in the year of retirement is often a more prudent choice.

> ***Disclosure:*** *Not associated with or endorsed by the Social Security Administration or any other government agency.*

IMPORTANT CONSIDERATIONS

- You become eligible for Social Security at age 62. However, if you retire between 62 and your Full Retirement Age, your benefit will be reduced. Additionally, there are limitations on earning outside income while receiving Social Security.
- Your full retirement age is typically around 66-67 depending on your birthdate. At this age, you can receive an unreduced benefit and work while

earning other income. However, retiring before your full retirement age may result in penalties, meaning you would have to give back some money. This is particularly important if you plan to do consulting or part-time work.

- Age 70 is the maximum age to claim Social Security, and there is no advantage to waiting beyond this age.
- Each year that you defer taking Social Security, your benefit grows by approximately 8% until age 70.
- Spouses can qualify for benefits in various ways, either using their own record or the higher-earning spouse's record. It's often surprising how much couples can receive together, up to 50% of the higher-earning spouse's benefit or their own record, whichever is higher.
- Social Security benefits are partially taxed, depending on several factors. Typically, you can expect to be taxed on 50% to 85% of your Social Security income, depending on your total yearly income. To simplify matters, consider setting up regular withholding or paying estimated quarterly taxes.
- Your Medicare premium will likely be deducted directly from your Social Security benefit.
- If you have children under the age of 18, they may qualify for their own benefit based on your record. Although this situation may be uncommon, it's worth noting.

DECIDING WHEN TO TAKE SOCIAL SECURITY

There is a strong argument for initiating Social Security (SS) at any age, emphasizing the significance of making a decision that aligns with your individual circumstances and needs.

THE CASE FOR CLAIMING SOCIAL SECURITY AT AGE 62

While delaying Social Security benefits can lead to larger monthly payments, choosing to claim at 62 might be the optimal decision for many individuals. The rationale for early claiming rests on several pillars:

- **IMMEDIATE FINANCIAL NEEDS:** If you're retiring early due to health issues or job loss, and you need income immediately, then claiming Social Security at 62 can help meet your financial needs. It can provide a critical safety net, ensuring you maintain your quality of life without draining your retirement savings prematurely.
- **HEALTH FACTORS:** If you have a shorter life expectancy due to health reasons, claiming early may mean receiving benefits over a longer period, assuming you live to your expected lifespan. Effectively, you could potentially receive more in total benefits than if you waited until full retirement age.

- **LIFESTYLE CHOICE:** Some people value their younger years in retirement more. If you want to enjoy your retirement while you're relatively young and healthy, taking Social Security at 62 can support a more active lifestyle early in retirement.

Consulting with a financial advisor can help ensure you make the best decision for your circumstances.

CASE FOR DELAYING SOCIAL SECURITY UNTIL AGE 70

Choosing to delay Social Security benefits until the age of 70 can be a strategic move, yielding long-term benefits that significantly outweigh the initial wait. The logic behind delaying rests on a variety of strategic considerations:

- **ENLARGED BENEFITS:** Each year you wait to claim Social Security beyond your full retirement age, your benefits increase by about 8% until age 70. This can result in significantly larger monthly payments, providing a substantial income stream in your later years.
- **LONGEVITY INSURANCE:** If you have a longer life expectancy, waiting to claim till 70 can provide you with a higher guaranteed income in your later years. This can be a form of *longevity insurance*, helping to ensure you don't outlive your retirement savings.

- **TAX CONSIDERATIONS:** If you continue to work in your 60s, claiming social security may push you into a higher tax bracket. By delaying social security, you can avoid higher taxes on your income.
- **SPOUSAL BENEFITS:** If you're the higher earner in a couple, your delayed retirement benefits can lead to higher survivor benefits for your spouse if you pass away first.

ASSESSING THE STRENGTH OF THE SOCIAL SECURITY RETIREMENT SYSTEM

The viability of the Social Security retirement system is a legitimate concern for many, particularly those nearing retirement age. It's important to note that Social Security is funded through payroll taxes, meaning as long as there are people working and paying taxes, funds will continue to flow into the system. However, demographic shifts such as the retirement of the baby boomer generation and declining birth rates are placing greater financial strain on the system.

According to the 2020 Social Security Trustees Report, the trust funds that disburse retirement benefits are projected to be depleted by 2035. If these reserves are exhausted and no action is taken to replenish them, the system will still be able to pay about 79% of scheduled benefits funded by incoming tax revenues.

These projections underscore the need for legislative measures to strengthen the long-term viability of the system. Potential solutions could include increasing payroll taxes, raising the retirement age, reducing future benefits, or a combination of these approaches.

While it's prudent to be aware of these issues, it's also important not to overreact. The Social Security retirement system has faced financial challenges in the past, and legislative actions have always been taken to address them. It's reasonable to assume that similar steps will be taken in the future to ensure the system's sustainability. Therefore, while concern is justified, it should be balanced with the understanding that in some form, Social Security is likely to remain a key component of retirement income for the foreseeable future.

As always, relying solely on Social Security for retirement income is not advised. It's essential to have a diversified retirement plan that includes personal savings, investments, and potentially employer-sponsored retirement plans. In this way, any future changes to the Social Security system will have a less dramatic impact on your overall retirement income.

LEGISLATIVE MEASURES TO SAVE THE SOCIAL SECURITY RETIREMENT SYSTEM

Several legislative measures could potentially bolster the Social Security retirement system, ensuring its sustainability well into the future. Here are some proposals lawmakers have considered:

- **INCREASING PAYROLL TAXES:** Currently, the Social Security payroll tax stands at 12.4%, split evenly between employers and employees. The tax applies only to income up to a certain limit, known as the taxable maximum, which is adjusted annually for inflation. One proposal is to raise the payroll tax rate or increase the taxable maximum, which would generate more revenue for the system.
- **RAISING THE RETIREMENT AGE:** Another commonly proposed solution is to increase the full retirement age, which is the age at which individuals become eligible to receive 100% of their benefits. Currently, the full retirement age is set to gradually reach 67 for those born in 1960 or later. Further raising the retirement age would result in fewer years of benefits for retirees, ultimately reducing the long-term costs of the system. It's worth noting that this adjustment would primarily impact future generations rather than your own.
- **MEANS-TESTING BENEFITS:** Under this proposal, Social Security benefits would be reduced or eliminated for high-income retirees, focusing more resources on low- and middle-income individuals. However, this option is often criticized as undermining the broad-based support for Social Security.

- **ADJUSTING THE BENEFITS FORMULA:** One way to reduce future benefits without breaking current retirees' promises would be to change the way the Social Security Administration calculates benefits. This could be achieved by adjusting the *bend points* in the benefit formula or changing the measure of inflation used to calculate the annual cost-of-living adjustment.
- **IMMIGRATION REFORM:** Increasing immigration, particularly of younger workers, could help alleviate some of the financial pressure on Social Security by broadening the base of taxpayers.
- **TYPES OF INCOME:** When considering Social Security, it is important to also examine the types of income that are allowed before reaching Full Retirement Age without affecting your benefits. Income from dividends, pensions, interest, and what I refer to as portfolio income is permissible, enabling individuals to receive as much income as they desire from most passive income sources and still receive their unpenalized retirement benefit. However, penalties are incurred on income earned from employment such as a job. This penalizes individuals for their productivity while overlooking unearned income.

These solutions are not mutually exclusive and could be combined in various ways to address the system's financial challenges. However, each involves trade-offs and would require careful consideration of their potential impacts on different groups of people. As such, public debate and political compromise will be necessary to ensure the long-term viability of the Social Security retirement system.

SUMMARY OF KEY POINTS

1. Eligibility for Social Security begins at 62 but claiming before Full Retirement Age results in reduced benefits.
2. Waiting until age 70 maximizes benefits, with an approximate 8% increase for each year delayed beyond FRA.
3. Considerations such as health, financial needs, and marital status impact the decision of when to claim Social Security.
4. Claiming early can provide necessary income for those in need or who prefer an early retirement lifestyle.
5. Delaying benefits offers financial advantages, including larger monthly payments and potential tax benefits, particularly for those with longer life expectancies or higher incomes.

CHAPTER 24

LONG-TERM CARE INSURANCE

Long-term care insurance provides coverage for extended care needs such as Alzheimer's disease, disabilities, or other medical conditions requiring prolonged care. This may encompass care in a nursing home or at home. The cost of such care can be exorbitant, with the national average for a private room in a nursing home estimated at $100,000 per year.

When should you start thinking about long-term care insurance? Once you reach the age of 65, there is a 50/50 probability that you will need some form of paid long-term care in your lifetime. The average total expense for such care is $140,000, as stated in an article by AARP.

- More than 95 percent of the claims are filed by individuals older than 70, as stated in an AARP article.
- The longer you delay obtaining LTC insurance, the greater the premium becomes.

- The optimal age range to explore purchasing a LTC policy is between 60 and 65.

Determining whether or not you require long-term care insurance is a deeply personal decision. It cannot be simplified into a broad statement of its overall merits or drawbacks. Even if you conclude that insurance is unnecessary, it remains crucial to have a well-thought-out plan in place for how long-term care costs could be covered.

MEDICARE, MEDICAID AND LONG-TERM CARE COSTS

Medicare does not cover long-term care expenses, leaving individuals responsible for paying out-of-pocket. Medicaid, on the other hand, may provide coverage but only if strict financial requirements are met. It is important to note that qualifying for Medicaid can be challenging, as you must have depleted your resources to near poverty levels. Eligibility criteria typically include being 65 years or older, visually impaired, disabled, having income below a certain threshold (around $3000 per month), and possessing assets below a specified limit (generally $2,000). It is worth mentioning that certain assets may be excluded based on individual circumstances and state regulations, such as home equity and specific personal property. Additionally, Medicaid conducts a five-year look back period to assess any asset transfers during that time period that they could claw back and use to pay for your long-term care.

LONG-TERM CARE OPTIONS

- **TRADITIONAL:** With this type of policy, you pay a monthly premium which can be subject to increases by the insurance company. On average, traditional LTC premiums amount to around $2,700 per year (according to an AARP article). Married couples who both obtain insurance may enjoy a discount of up to 30%. However, many insurance carriers have faced challenges with this type of coverage. While over 100 carriers offered it in the 1990s, today there are fewer than 15. These policies have a track record of premium hikes and losses for insurance companies due to inaccurate cost forecasts for providing care.
- **HYBRID:** These policies offer a convenient option where you pay a single premium, usually a substantial amount like $100,000. The key advantage is that the insurance company cannot increase the premium. Despite the upfront cost, you have the flexibility to cancel the policy and receive a refund. Alternatively, if you require long-term care (LTC), the policy provides specific benefits based on your underwriting. In the event of your passing without utilizing LTC or exhausting benefits equal to your original premium, your beneficiaries will inherit the remaining amount. It's worth considering the opportunity cost of this policy, as the premium cannot be invested. However, one could argue that this money is actively safeguarding and protecting you.

Key components of a long-term care policy include:

- **ELIMINATION PERIOD:** This refers to a specific number of days, usually around 90 days, during which you must be in a long-term care facility before the policy starts covering the costs.
- **DAILY BENEFIT MAXIMUM:** This represents the maximum amount the policy will pay per day for your long-term care expenses.
- **MONTHLY BENEFIT MAXIMUM:** This indicates the maximum monthly amount that the policy will cover for your long-term care needs.
- **LIFETIME MAXIMUM:** This represents the maximum total amount that the policy will pay over your lifetime for long-term care services.
- **INFLATION PROTECTION:** This feature ensures that the coverage amount adjusts over time to account for inflation, allowing your policy to keep pace with rising long-term care costs.

Instead of purchasing LTC insurance, you have the option to self-insure. Take a moment to consider how you will cover the costs of LTC if the need arises. Is your income sufficient to redirect funds towards LTC expenses? Do you possess home equity that could serve as a backup plan? Additionally, do you have a reserve account in place, such as the one we recommend in a *Time-Segmented Strategy*?

Reducing the likelihood of requiring long-term care is critical. As Benjamin Franklin wisely said, "An ounce of prevention is worth a pound of cure." This rings especially true when it comes to long-term care. According to the US Department of Health and Human Services, the need for such services often stems from falls. By preventing falls, you can potentially delay or even avoid the need for long-term care in your own life or that of your spouse. I've included an entire section later in this book on living a "Fall Free" retirement.

What about using trusts and estate planning to shift assets and qualify for Medicaid? Depending on the state, these strategies can be quite effective in transferring assets to preserve them from Medicaid's estate recovery program. In some cases, the right setup may also protect you from losing your home and other valuable possessions. Consulting with a lawyer is important since this involves complex legal instruments such as irrevocable trusts and annuities. It is essential to understand the trade-offs and potential risks involved in these strategies. The earlier you plan, the more options you have at your disposal.

SUMMARY OF KEY POINTS

- **MEDICAID ELIGIBILITY:** To qualify for Medicaid, individuals must have income below approximately $3,000 per month and assets under $2,000, excluding some assets like home equity depending on state regulations. A five-year lookback period checks for asset transfers that could impact eligibility.
- **LONG-TERM CARE INSURANCE OPTIONS:** Consumers can choose between traditional policies with annual premiums and potential rate hikes, and hybrid policies with a one-time premium but no rate increase risk. Both have advantages and limitations, including coverage features like daily and lifetime maximums, elimination periods, and inflation protection.
- **SELF-INSURANCE FOR LONG-TERM CARE:** Instead of purchasing insurance, individuals may consider self-insuring for long-term care, utilizing income, home equity, or savings. Preparing for such scenarios involves a significant financial strategy and works with a *Time-Segmented Strategy*.

- **PREVENTETIVE MEASURES TO REDUCE LONG-TERM CARE RISKS:** Engaging in fall prevention strategies and lifestyle adjustments can significantly lower the need for long-term care. Keeping living spaces safe and opting for smaller pets to avoid tripping hazards may help avoid accidents and consequent care requirements.
- **ASSET PROTECTION AND ESTATE PLANNING:** Using trusts and estate planning can help individuals qualify for Medicaid while preserving assets from estate recovery. Early planning with legal advice is critical to understand the complexities of irrevocable trusts and annuities for asset protection.

CHAPTER 25

EFFECTIVE RETIREMENT SPENDING STRATEGIES

SPENDING IN RETIREMENT/BUDGETING

When people approach me for retirement planning advice, they often inquire about budgeting. However, instead of focusing solely on expenses, it is more valuable to consider income. By understanding your income, you can shape your lifestyle accordingly and create a budget that aligns with your earnings. This could be called *Reverse Budgeting*. Remember, it's easier to adjust your spending to fit your income than to create an income that fits your budget. But first, you must have a clear understanding of your income. Budgeting without this knowledge isn't effective.

Budgets can be compared to diets, as many of them fail to deliver the desired results. Our spending habits are influenced by a mix of good and bad habits, as well as our self-perception, which carries its own expenses. We naturally adapt our lives based on the resources available to us. If budgeting comes naturally to you, it can provide a sense of freedom by establishing a clear picture of your income and expenditures.

PLANNING YOUR RETIREMENT SPENDING

When planning your retirement spending, it's important to consider the following factors:

Typically, experts suggest that retirees will spend around 70-100% of their pre-retirement income. However, keep in mind that your spending may vary during different stages of retirement. For instance, you may prioritize travel and activities during the first decade of retirement while you still have the physical energy and health to fully enjoy them. This may result in higher spending during the early years, followed by a gradual reduction in later years. You can structure your retirement around these different spending levels by categorizing them into four themes: *transition*, *active*, *less active*, and *later*.

THE PHASES OF RETIREMENT SPENDING

Retirement is not a static state, but rather an ever-evolving journey that unfolds through different phases. Understanding these phases can greatly assist in making sound retirement planning decisions. The three primary phases of retirement spending can be described as the *Go-Go Years*, the *Slow-Go Years*, and the *No-Go Years*.

- **THE *GO-GO* YEARS** symbolize the initial stage of retirement, brimming with excitement, freedom, and activity. Typically spanning around 10-15 years, this phase is characterized by a vibrant and energetic lifestyle.
- **THE *SLOW-GO* YEARS** mark the transition into a more relaxed and leisurely lifestyle, where expenses may naturally slow down as individuals grow older.
- **THE *NO-GO* YEARS** represent a phase in retirement where activities may be limited due to health reasons, and the focus shifts toward healthcare and support services.

By thoughtfully considering these factors and adjusting financial plans accordingly, individuals can enhance their retirement experience and fully embrace this new chapter of life. While it can be argued that travel expenses may decrease as one ages, it is important to acknowledge the potential increase in healthcare costs.

CREATIVE BUDGETING IDEAS

One of my favorite retirement budgeting ideas is to create *Freedom Funds*—special accounts dedicated to enjoyable activities such as travel. By segregating this money from your retirement plan, you can indulge without feeling guilty. For example, you can allocate $50,000 into five separate funds, enabling you to embark on five $10,000 trips during the initial years of retirement. Doesn't that sound alluring?

SUMMARY OF KEY POINTS

- Avoid fixating solely on your retirement budget.
- Instead, conduct *Reverse Budgeting* by focusing on what your income levels will be and adjust accordingly.
- Tailor your retirement income plan to fit your specific life stages: *Go-Go*, *Slow-Go*, and *No-Go*.
- Explore *Freedom Funds* as a guilt-free source for enjoying leisure activities without impacting your overall financial plan.
- Expect to spend around 70-100% of your pre-retirement expenses, as some costs may shift but won't completely disappear. Be prepared for new expenses to arise.

CHAPTER 26

PENSION OPTIONS

Pensions are designed to provide a dependable stream of retirement income that is guaranteed to last throughout your lifetime. Unlike investments tied to the stock market, pensions offer a secure source of income that is not subject to market volatility. In some cases, the income from pensions can be tailored and personalized within certain limits. It is important to familiarize yourself with the key features of pensions.

In recent years, many companies have phased out pension plans due to their high costs. Instead, they are now offering lump sum buyouts to employees before retirement, in order to transfer their pension obligations. If you have a pension, you will need to carefully consider whether a lifetime income or a lump-sum payout is the better option. To make an informed decision, there are several important aspects of pensions of which you should be aware.

CONSIDERING A LUMP SUM BUYOUT

If you have a pension, you may receive a buyout offer before or during retirement. As an expert in pension evaluations, I regularly review these offers and find that they can vary significantly. There is no one-size-fits-all answer to determine the best choice.

To assess the value of a lump-sum buyout offer, a quick method is to compare the cost of creating an equivalent income through purchasing a guaranteed lifetime annuity on the private market. This comparison will promptly reveal if the buyout is a fair deal based on the current market conditions.

Furthermore, it's worth considering the potential income you could generate with your own income strategy if you opt for the lump sum rather than the pension income.

There are both advantages and disadvantages to consider when weighing your options. Opting for a lump sum payout offers the advantage of having control over your money. It can provide a significant boost to your retirement savings, often unexpectedly. However, accepting a lump sum requires careful planning to avoid immediate taxation on the entire amount.

To avoid paying taxes all at once, you can typically roll the money into a *Traditional IRA*, deferring taxation until you make withdrawals from the IRA. While you will eventually pay taxes when you withdraw all the money, doing so on your own terms allows for greater flexibility and the opportunity to spread the tax burden over a longer period.

On the other hand, the downside of taking a lump sum is assuming the responsibility of managing the money yourself. Previously, the pension provider, often an insurance company, bore the risk of ensuring a lifetime income for you. Now, that responsibility will fall on your shoulders. While you gain control and flexibility, you also assume the prudent management of these funds.

WHAT YOU SHOULD KNOW ABOUT YOUR PENSION

Cost Of Living Adjustment (COLA)

Pensions can hold great value due to their ability to provide a guaranteed lifetime income, particularly when accompanied by a cost-of-living adjustment (COLA). A COLA ensures that your pension payment increases annually to keep pace with rising costs and inflation. This safeguard preserves the purchasing power of your pension, ensuring a comfortable standard of living throughout retirement. While such a valuable feature is rare, it is commonly found in government pensions for Federal and State employees.

COMMON PAYOUT OPTIONS

There are different types of pension options to consider:

1. **LIFE ONLY:** This option provides payments for your lifetime. However, once you pass away, the payments stop. While this option usually offers the highest amount, it only covers your life.

2. **JOINT AND SURVIVOR:** With this option, you receive payments for your lifetime and also for the lifetime of another person, such as a spouse.

3. **LIFE WITH PERIOD CERTAIN:** This option provides payments for your lifetime and guarantees a minimum period, such as 10 years, from the start date. It offers some protection to your beneficiaries. If you were to pass away within a few years, the payments would continue for the remaining number of years specified.

4. **LIFE AND 50% SURVIVOR:** This option pays you for life and provides your beneficiaries with payments equal to 50% of what you were receiving.

5. **PLOP:** This option involves receiving a partial lump sum upfront and a lifetime income. It allows you to access a significant sum of money initially and provides a regular income. This option is commonly found in 403b plans.

Take the time to carefully evaluate these pension options, ensuring they align with your needs and financial objectives. Now, when it comes to determining the ideal choice, just like pensions themselves, there isn't a one-size-fits-all answer. It's crucial to conduct your own analysis but allow me to provide some guidance.

PENSION CONSIDERATIONS

- A pension with a COLA is a positive indicator of its quality.
- For married individuals, opting for a 100% survivor benefit seems appealing. After all, when one passes away, household expenses are unlikely to be halved. It's prudent to ensure that income streams are not cut in half if possible. The tradeoff for adding a beneficiary payout is often minimal, meaning it doesn't significantly reduce overall income while ensuring continued income for both lives.
- If you are single with no dependents relying on you, a life-only pension may be worth considering. This option maximizes your pension income.
- There are instances where choosing a lump sum is the best choice. This occurs when you can leverage the cash lump sum to generate more flexible and potentially higher income than what the pension offers. However, it's important to have a retirement income plan in place to assess how things would look with either the pension or the lump sum.

Making the right decision regarding a pension can be more complex than anticipated. However, while it may seem challenging, it doesn't have to be excessively difficult. What if the company responsible for the pension encounters unforeseen circumstances?

SUMMARY OF KEY POINTS

- Recognize the true value of your pension. It may be more valuable than you think.
- If you are offered a lump sum buyout, understand that the employer benefits from your acceptance due to cost savings. However, carefully consider the offer before making a decision.
- If the pension company proposes a lump sum payment, don't rush into accepting it without conducting a proper analysis.
- For married individuals choosing lifetime income, prioritize your spouse's financial security by considering a 50-100% survivor benefit. Opting for a 100% benefit is ideal, as expenses won't be halved if you pass away, and you wouldn't want your spouse's income to be reduced, either.
- When accepting a lump sum, avoid simply depositing the check into your bank account. The taxes on the distribution can be surprisingly high, as it's likely taxed at your regular income rate, which is higher. Instead, roll the money into a *Traditional IRA* to manage taxes and continue using it for retirement, only paying taxes on the necessary amount.

CHAPTER 27

ESTATE PLANNING

Estate Planning is often portrayed as complex, but it is just a process that makes sure your assets are distributed according to your wishes after you pass away. It simply involves aligning the manner and timeframe of distribution with your desires.

UNDERSTANDING ESTATE PLANNING

At its core, estate planning is a way to make sure that your assets are distributed the way you want them to be after you pass away. It also allows your heirs to minimize taxes and other costs associated with transferring wealth, maximize value of your estate, and potentially even save on probate fees.

KEY ELEMENTS OF ESTATE PLANNING

1. **LIVING WILL AND HEALTHCARE DIRECTIVE:** These documents specify your preferences for medical care if you're unable to communicate them yourself. They are essential for ensuring that your healthcare wishes are known and respected.

2. **POWER OF ATTORNEY:** This allows you to appoint someone to make financial and other decisions on your behalf if you become incapacitated.

3. **FUNERAL ARRANGEMENTS:** You can outline your wishes for your funeral service and burial or cremation, relieving your loved ones of the burden of making these decisions during a difficult time.

4. **A WILL OR TRUST:** These documents are crucial for specifying how your assets should be distributed after your death. A trust can also help manage specific assets and avoid probate.

5. **GUARDIANSHIP FOR MINOR CHILDREN:** If you have minor children, it's essential to appoint a guardian in your will or estate plan, ensuring they are cared for by someone you trust.

KEEPING YOUR PLAN SIMPLE

Estate planning doesn't have to be complicated. Even if you're unsure or pressed for time, there are simple steps you can take now to make a difference in the future. One initial action is to add beneficiaries to all your accounts, whether they're retirement or non-retirement accounts. This straightforward step helps ensure the proper allocation of assets, especially if you don't have a will or trust.

To maximize the benefits, consider managing real estate and other specific assets through a trust. A key aspect of estate planning is establishing a will or trust, which guarantees the seamless transfer of your assets to the individuals you designate after your passing. By taking this crucial step, you can have peace of mind knowing that your wishes will be fulfilled, providing security for you and your loved ones.

If your estate is particularly large, it may be prudent to explore a more comprehensive plan. This could involve establishing multiple trusts or revocable living trusts, along with other intricate arrangements tailored to each beneficiary's desired outcome and tax situation. Additionally, for those with minor children, it is crucial to create a legal document appointing a guardian for them. This task can often be addressed when drafting your will, trust, or other estate planning documents.

THE ROLE OF PROFESSIONALS IN ESTATE PLANNING

When seeking assistance with estate planning, there are numerous qualified professionals available to help you develop a personalized plan that meets your specific needs. These professionals, including attorneys and financial advisors can offer invaluable guidance and support in managing your estate. While attorneys typically handle the creation of essential documents such as wills or trusts, other advisors can contribute to shaping your comprehensive strategy.

THE COST OF ESTATE PLANNING

The cost of estate planning can vary significantly depending on the extent and intricacy of your plan. For instance, setting up a basic will or trust can be relatively affordable, ranging from a few hundred to several thousand dollars. However, more intricate packages may involve costs in the thousands of dollars. It's important to note that ongoing advice from a financial advisor may also require an annual fee.

CONSEQUENCES OF NOT HAVING AN ESTATE PLAN

Failing to have an estate plan in place can have significant consequences upon your passing. Without a will or trust, state laws and intestate succession may dictate the distribution of your assets, potentially conflicting with your wishes. Moreover, probate fees and taxes can substantially deplete the estate, resulting in heirs not receiving their rightful inheritance.

To ensure a seamless transition and a secure future for your loved ones, it is vital to have a well-crafted estate plan. By seeking guidance from qualified professionals and carefully considering your individual circumstances, you can create a comprehensive plan that preserves your legacy for generations to come.

SUMMARY OF KEY POINTS

- Estate planning is the strategic process of ensuring that your assets and wealth are distributed according to your wishes upon your demise, aiming to minimize taxes, maximize the estate's value for heirs, and potentially save on probate fees. Key elements of an estate plan include a living will, power of attorney, and instructions about care preferences and funeral arrangements.
- Initial steps towards effective estate planning include adding beneficiaries to all your accounts and managing specific assets like real estate through a trust. For larger estates, a comprehensive plan involving multiple trusts and intricate arrangements may be necessary. If minor children are involved, a legal document appointing a guardian should be created.

- The cost of estate planning varies based on its extent and complexity, with basic plans being affordable and more intricate plans costing thousands of dollars. Without a proper estate plan, state laws may dictate the distribution of your assets, potentially conflicting with your wishes, and probate fees and taxes could significantly deplete the estate's value. Thus, creating a comprehensive estate plan with professional guidance is essential.

CHAPATER 28

NAVIGATING HEALTH INSURANCE IN RETIREMENT

One of the less discussed yet crucial aspects of planning for early retirement is managing health insurance expenses before qualifying for Medicare at age 65. This chapter seeks to shed light on the importance of strategic health insurance planning and the various options available to ensure retirees can transition smoothly into their next phase of life without financial strain due to healthcare costs.

UNDERSTANDING YOUR OPTIONS BEFORE MEDICARE ELIGIBILITY

Having a well-thought-out plan for financing health insurance before Medicare is crucial. If you're retiring before the age of 65, it's important to arrange your own insurance coverage. Some companies may offer the option to continue on their insurance for a limited period known as COBRA. However, it's worth noting that the cost is likely to be higher compared to when you were a full-time employee.

If COBRA is not available or has expired, you may need to secure insurance through the health exchange. The cost can vary depending on your income levels, potentially resulting in higher expenses. However, once you turn 65, you become eligible for Medicare, which often leads to significant savings in monthly premiums.

STRATEGIES OFR PAYING HEALTH INSURANCE PREMIUMS

There are strategies to consider when paying for health insurance premiums during retirement. Many retirees are pleasantly surprised by how effectively they can bridge the gap to age 65 without significant impact on their overall financial plan. I've noticed that engaging in strategic planning and making premium payments for a few brief years has minimal impact on their anticipated lifetime income generated from their resources. In fact, they often feel relieved and grateful that they didn't delay until 65 based on a perceived necessity. They discover that they can achieve their retirement goals without sacrificing financial stability.

Here's a recommended strategy for retirees:

- First, explore the possibility of being included in your spouse's insurance if they are still employed.

- Next, examine the details of COBRA, such as associated costs and accessibility duration.
- Lastly, consider researching private insurance options to determine the cost.

Once the estimated costs are determined, they should be incorporated into the retiree's overall retirement budget. The budget for the years leading up to turning 65 should include provisions for these additional expenses. It may be necessary to make adjustments to accommodate these extra costs.

By adopting this approach, you can proactively plan for health insurance coverage during the transitional period, ensuring a smooth and financially secure retirement. Here are some key steps to consider when approaching health insurance during retirement:

1. **THOROUGHLY RESEARCH YOUR OPTIONS:** Gain a comprehensive understanding of the different types of insurance available to you. This may involve exploring employer-sponsored plans, COBRA, or private insurance. Each option has its own advantages and disadvantages in terms of cost, coverage, and provider networks.

2. **CONSIDER YOUR HEALTH NEEDS:** Take into account your current health status and any anticipated future needs. If you have chronic conditions or require regular medical care, it may be worth paying a higher premium for a plan that offers lower out-of-pocket costs.

3. **STAY INFORMED ON POLICY CHANGES:** Health insurance laws and regulations can change over time, potentially affecting your coverage or costs. Stay up to date with any legislative changes that may impact your insurance.

4. **SEEK EXPERT ADVICE:** Consulting with professionals in the field can provide valuable guidance and expertise to help you make informed decisions about your health insurance coverage.

By following these steps, retirees can navigate the complexities of health insurance and ensure they have the coverage they need to enjoy a secure and worry-free retirement.

SUMMARY OF KEY POINTS

- **PRE-MEDICARE PLANNING IS CRITICAL:** Don't wait until retirement to understand your health insurance options. Start early to ensure a seamless transition.
- **EXPLORE ALL OPTIONS:** From COBRA to private insurance, comprehensively research what's available to you.
- **INCORPORATE COSTS INTO YOUR BUDGET:** Ensure that your retirement budget realistically includes health insurance premiums and potential out-of-pocket expenses.

- **STAY INFORMED:** Health insurance policies and costs can change. Keeping abreast of these changes can save you from future surprises.
- **SEEK PROFESSIONAL ADVICE:** Consulting with financial or insurance experts can provide insights tailored to your personal situation and needs, ensuring that you make the best decisions concerning your health insurance in retirement.

CHAPTER 29

CONSIDERATIONS WHEN MAKING DECISIONS ABOUT MEDICARE

Medicare is a federal health insurance program in the United States that provides coverage for people aged 65 or older, certain younger people with disabilities, and people with End-Stage Renal Disease (permanent kidney failure requiring dialysis or a transplant). It was established in 1965 during the presidency of Lyndon B. Johnson as part of his *Great Society* vision.

The creation of Medicare was a monumental breakthrough in American social policy. Before its inception, only half of the older adult population in the U.S. had health insurance, and they paid three times as much for it as younger people. The goal of Medicare was to address this issue by providing affordable, accessible health care coverage to the senior population. This was particularly important given that the older population often has more health-related needs and costs. Today, Medicare continues to be a vital lifeline for many senior Americans, helping to cover the cost of various health care services, including hospital stays, physician visits, prescription drugs, preventive services, and more.

There are several key points retirees should understand about Medicare:

- **ELIGIBILITY:** Most people are eligible for Medicare when they turn 65. However, younger people with disabilities and those with End-Stage Renal Disease are also eligible.
- **PARTS OF MEDICARE:** Medicare is divided into four parts: *Part A (Hospital Insurance)*, *Part B (Medical Insurance)*, *Part C (Medicare Advantage)*, and *Part D (Prescription Drug Coverage)*. Each part covers different health care services.
- **ENROLLMENT:** Initial enrollment for Medicare begins three months before you turn 65 and ends three months after. If you miss this initial enrollment period, there's a general enrollment period from January 1 through March 31 each year.
- **COSTS:** Most people don't pay a premium for *Part A*, but there are premiums for *Part B* and *Part D*. Costs vary depending on income level, the *Part D* plan chosen, and whether or not you're enrolled in a *Part C* plan.

- **SUPPLEMENTAL COVERAGE:** *Medicare Supplement Insurance (Medigap)* can help pay for costs not covered by *Original Medicare*, like copayments, coinsurance, and deductibles.
- **PRESCRIPTION DRUGS:** *Medicare Part D* provides prescription drug coverage. Each *Part D* plan has its own list of covered drugs, known as a formulary, and may place drugs into different tiers on their formularies.
- **PROVIDER CHOICES:** Depending on whether you choose *Original Medicare* or a *Medicare Advantage Plan*, you may have restrictions on which doctors and hospitals you can use.

Medicare Part B premiums can vary year by year and are determined based on your income. As of 2024, the standard *Part B* premium is $174.70 per month. However, if your modified adjusted gross income (MAGI) as reported on your IRS tax return from two years ago is above a certain amount, you may pay an *Income Related Monthly Adjustment Amount (IRMAA)*, which is an extra charge added to your premium. The payment is usually deducted from your Social Security, Railroad Retirement, or Civil Service Retirement payment. If these payments are not sufficient to cover the premium, or you do not have these retirement benefits, you will receive a bill from Medicare.

Choosing a *Medicare Advantage* plan over regular *Medicare* can offer several benefits, depending on an individual's specific healthcare needs and budget considerations.

1. **ALL-INCLUSIVE COVERAGE:** *Medicare Advantage* plans, often known as *Part C*, are offered by private insurance companies approved by Medicare. These plans include all benefits and services covered under *Part A* and *Part B* and usually include prescription drug coverage as well, which under regular Medicare would require enrolling in a separate *Part D* plan.

2. **EXTRA BENEFITS:** Some *Medicare Advantage* plans offer additional benefits that *Original Medicare* doesn't cover, such as dental, hearing, vision, and sometimes wellness programs like gym memberships.

3. **COST-SAVING POTENTIAL:** Depending on the plan, a *Medicare Advantage* user might pay a lower copayment for medical services. Some plans offer a yearly limit on your out-of-pocket costs. Once you reach a certain limit, you'll pay nothing for covered services for the rest of the year.

4. **CONVENIENCE:** With a *Medicare Advantage* plan, all your coverage options are bundled into one plan, which can make managing your benefits and handling paperwork easier.

However, it's important to note that while *Medicare Advantage* plans can offer significant advantages, they also come with certain limitations. For example, these plans may limit your coverage to a network of doctors and hospitals. It's crucial to understand all aspects of these plans before making a decision.

To get a *Medicare Advantage* plan, it's a multi-step process that involves a level of decision-making and analysis. Here are the steps in simplified form:

1. **CHECK YOUR ELIGIBILITY**: To be eligible for a *Medicare Advantage* plan, you must have *Medicare Parts A* and *B*, and live in the plan's service area.

2. **RESEARCH**: Start by researching the different *Medicare Advantage* plans in your area. Use the *Medicare Plan Finder* on *Medicare.gov* to see all the available options. Each plan has different out-of-pocket costs and rules for how you get services.

3. **COMPARE**: Consider the benefits (like dental, vision, or prescription drug coverage), the network of doctors and hospitals, the out-of-pocket costs, and the plan's rating.

4. **ENROLL**: Once you've chosen a plan, you can enroll during certain times of the year. You can enroll when you first become eligible for *Medicare* (Initial Enrollment Period), during the fall (Annual Enrollment Period), or during a Special Enrollment Period if you qualify. You can enroll through the plan's website, by calling the plan directly, or by calling 1-800-MEDICARE.

5. **REVIEW**: It's important to review your plan each year during the annual enrollment period. Your plan's costs or benefits may change from year to year.

Remember, you can switch your plan or go back to *Original Medicare* (and join a *Prescription Drug* plan) once during the first three months of the year if you're in a *Medicare Advantage* plan.

There are several resources available to help you navigate the *Medicare* enrollment process:

- **MEDICARE.GOV:** This is the official U.S. government site for *Medicare* where you can find comprehensive information about *Medicare* plans, coverage, and costs. Their online tools can help you compare plans and find local help.
- **STATE HEALTH INSURANCE ASSISTANCE PROGRAMS (SHIPs)**: These programs offer free, in-depth, one-on-one insurance counseling and assistance to *Medicare* beneficiaries, their families, friends, and caregivers. SHIPs operate in all 50 states, the District of Columbia, Guam, Puerto Rico, and the U.S. Virgin Islands.
- **SOCIAL SECURITY ADMINISTRATION:** If you're already getting benefits from Social Security or the Railroad Retirement Board (RRB), you'll automatically be enrolled in *Original Medicare (Parts A and B).* You can also apply for *Medicare* through Social Security if you're close to 65 but not getting Social Security or Railroad Retirement Board (RRB) benefits.

- **ELDERCARE LOCATOR:** This public service of the *U.S. Administration on Aging* connects you to services for older adults and their families. They can provide guidance and support as you navigate *Medicare*.

Remember, it's essential to seek help from trusted sources when enrolling in *Medicare*. Be wary of anyone who contacts you unsolicited about *Medicare* plans, as these could be scams. Always double-check any information you receive.

Many retirees often face unexpected discoveries when it comes to *Medicare*. Here are a few common surprises:

COMMON SURPRISES ABOUT MEDICARE

1. **MEDICARE IS NOT FREE:** Some retirees are surprised to learn that *Medicare* is not free. While *Part A*, which covers hospital services, typically doesn't have a premium, *Parts B* (medical insurance) and *D* (prescription drugs) do.

2. **NOT ALL SERVICES ARE COVERED:** Another common misconception is that *Medicare* covers all health services. However, it does not cover certain services like long-term care, dental care, eye examinations related to prescribing glasses, and more.

3. **LATE ENROLLMENT PENALTIES:** If you don't sign up for *Medicare Part B* when you're first eligible, you might have to pay a late enrollment penalty for as long as you have *Part B*. The penalty increases the longer you go without *Part B* coverage.

4. **OUT-OF-POCKET COSTS CAN BE HIGH:** Even with Medicare, out-of-pocket costs can still be substantial. These costs can include deductibles, copayments, and other expenses not covered by *Medicare*.

5. **LACK OF LONG-TERM CARE COVERAGE:** One glaring omission in *Medicare* coverage is long-term care. Despite widespread belief, *Medicare* does not cover the costs of long-term services such as nursing homes or assisted living facilities. These services, often necessary for individuals with chronic illnesses, disabilities, or recovery from a major illness, can incur substantial costs. This gap in coverage underscores the importance of planning for potential long-term care needs separately, either through personal savings or purchasing long-term care insurance.

6. **THE COMPLEXITY**: Many retirees are surprised by how complicated *Medicare* can be. With various parts and plans, enrollment periods, and coverage rules, navigating Medicare can be daunting.

CHAPTER 30

EARLY EXIT—THE CHALLENGES OF RETIRING BEFORE AGE 62

Opting for early retirement before the age of 62 is a dream for many, yet it brings with it a unique set of challenges that demands meticulous planning and consideration. The key to a successful early retirement lies in understanding and preparing for these challenges ahead of time. In this chapter, we'll explore the special considerations you need to address if you're contemplating retiring before the conventional age of 62.

FINANCIAL PREPAREDNESS

The cornerstone of early retirement is financial preparedness. Retiring early means you'll need your savings to last longer, highlighting the importance of a substantial retirement nest egg. A strategic withdrawal plan is essential to avoid running through your savings too quickly, especially during the initial years which tend to be more financially demanding without the cushion of investment growth.

HEALTHCARE COVERAGE

One of the biggest considerations for early retirees is healthcare. Losing employer-sponsored health insurance means you'll need to bridge the gap until Medicare kicks in at age 65. Finding comprehensive and affordable health insurance during this gap is critical to protect yourself against unforeseen medical expenses.

SOCIAL SECURITY BENEFITS

Social Security provides a safety net for many retirees, but if you retire before age 62, you'll need to plan for a period without these benefits. While you can start claiming Social Security at 62, doing so results in reduced payments. Effective planning is needed to smoothly transition to this phase of your retirement income.

IMPACT OF INFLATION

Inflation is a silent thief that can erode the purchasing power of your retirement funds over time. Early retirees face a longer exposure to inflation risks, making it essential to incorporate inflationary impacts into your retirement planning. This ensures that your savings continue to meet your living needs throughout retirement.

STRATEGIC WITHDRAWALS FROM RETIREMENT ACCOUNTS

Accessing funds from your IRA before the age of 59-1/2 typically incurs a 10% penalty. However, with smart planning, there are ways to bypass this penalty. Understanding and leveraging these strategies can significantly mitigate the financial impacts of early withdrawals, preserving your retirement savings.

By carefully considering these factors and regularly reviewing and adjusting your retirement plan, you can ensure a financially confident and fulfilling early retirement. The path to retiring early is filled with excitement and challenges, but with the right preparation, it can lead to a rewarding and enriching phase of your life.

1. **FINANCIAL PREPAREDNESS**: A significant retirement nest egg and a strategic withdrawal plan are vital for sustaining an early retirement, emphasizing the necessity to manage savings meticulously to cover a potentially longer retirement period.

2. **HEALTHCARE COVERAGE**: Securing comprehensive and affordable healthcare coverage is crucial for bridging the gap until Medicare eligibility, mitigating the risk of unexpected medical expenses.

3. **SOCIAL SECURITY BENEFITS**: Early retirees must plan for a duration without Social Security benefits, considering the reduction in payments if benefits are claimed before reaching the full retirement age.

4. **IMPACT OF INFLATION**: Incorporating inflationary impacts into retirement planning is essential to preserve the purchasing power of retirement funds, given the longer exposure period due to early retirement.

5. **STRATEGIC WITHDRAWALS FROM RETIREMENT ACCOUNTS**: Understanding and leveraging strategies to avoid penalties on early withdrawals from retirement accounts can help preserve retirement savings and support financial stability during early retirement.

PART V

LIVING YOUR BEST LIFE IN RETIREMENT

CHAPTER 31

WHAT'S IMPORTANT TO YOU—DEFINING YOUR PERSONAL VALUES

UNDERSTANDING THE IMPORTANCE OF PERSONAL VALUES IN RETIRMENT PLANNING

As you embark on the journey of retirement it becomes critical to understand and define your personal values. These values serve as guiding principles that shape your aspirations, behaviors, and priorities in life. By defining your values, you can make better financial decisions that align with your core. Such decisions are likely to be rational, less emotional, and ultimately wiser choices.

INITIATING THE CONVERSATION FOR MARRIED COUPLES

Start by having an open discussion with your spouse about what truly matters to you both. This could include values like family, health, independence, learning, adventure, or service to others. Remember, there are no right or wrong answers here. What's important is that these values resonate deeply with you and represent what you believe to be meaningful in life.

REFLECTING ON PAST EXPERIENCES

Consider past experiences and life decisions that have brought you happiness, fulfillment, or a sense of accomplishment. Often, these experiences reflect our core values. Similarly, consider situations that have caused dissatisfaction or discomfort, as they might indicate values that were compromised.

RESPECTING INDIVIDUAL DIFFERENCES

Understand that each individual may have distinct values and it's perfectly normal. The key is to respect each other's values and find common ground where possible, which can strengthen your bond and mutual understanding.

ALIGNING VALUES WITH RETIREMENT PLANS

Once you've identified these values, try to align them with your retirement plans. For example, if health is a priority, incorporate regular exercise and a balanced diet into your retirement lifestyle. If lifelong learning is important, consider enrolling in courses or visiting museums and historical sites.

THE CONTINUOUS JOURNEY OF DEFINING PERSONAL VALUES

Defining personal values is a continuous, evolving process that requires introspection and honest communication. Embracing this process can lead to a more purposeful, enriching, and satisfying retirement for you and your spouse.

SUMMARY OF KEY POINTS

- **THE SIGNIFICANCE OF PERSONAL VALUES:** Define and understand your values to make better, more aligned financial decisions during retirement.
- **STARTING THE CONVERSATION:** Engage in open discussions about what matters most, reflecting on past experiences for deeper insights.
- **INDIVIDUAL VALUES IN A SHARED LIFE:** Respect and understand each partner's unique values, seeking common ground for a unified approach.

- **ALIGNING VALUES WITH RETIREMENT PLANNING:** Integrate your core values into your retirement plans to ensure a fulfilling retirement lifestyle.
- **AN EVOLVING JOURNEY:** Continuously reflect on and adapt your values, understanding that this is an ongoing process critical for a rewarding retirement experience.

CHAPTER 32

ALIGNING FINANCIAL DECISIONS WITH FAMILY VALUES IN RETIREMENT

THE POWER OF SHARED VALUES

Aligning financial decisions with your family values in retirement has far-reaching benefits that extend beyond monetary gains. This approach fosters unity, understanding, and respect within the family, as it ensures that financial decisions are made with everyone's values and aspirations in mind.

For instance, if philanthropy is a shared family value, setting aside a portion of your retirement fund for charitable contributions can engender a sense of fulfillment and purpose. It not only benefits the recipients of your generosity but also deepens your family's bond through shared commitments to causes about which you collectively care.

Education as a fundamental value within your family is a valid reason to support your grandchildren financially in their college journeys. On the other hand, it may not be in line with your values to contribute toward buying them a new car at the age of 16.

IMPACT ON LEGACY PLANNING

Aligning financial decisions with family values also plays a crucial role in legacy planning. It can help ensure that your wealth is passed on in a way that honors your family's values and supports the causes, initiatives, or investments you hold dear.

PRUDENT AND MEANINGFUL SPENDING

Moreover, this alignment can lead to more prudent and meaningful spending. If sustainability is a family value, for instance, you might choose to invest in eco-friendly products or services which can have long-term benefits for both your wallet and the environment.

FINANCIAL SATISFACTION AND PEACE OF MIND

Lastly, when financial decisions reflect family values, it can contribute to greater financial satisfaction and peace of mind. Knowing that your money is allocated in ways that resonate with your family's values will provide a priceless sense of fulfillment.

THE IMPORTANCE OF COMMUNICATION

Aligning financial decisions with family values necessitates open and honest family discussions about both money and values. Although these conversations can be challenging, they are a crucial step towards crafting a financial road map that embodies the values and principles that define your family.

SUMMARY OF KEY POINTS

- **SHARED VALUES ENHANCE FAMILY UNITY**: Making financial decisions based on shared family values, such as philanthropy or education, strengthens the family bond and fosters mutual respect.
- **SUPPORTING MEANINGFUL CAUSES**: Allocating retirement funds to causes important to the family, like charity or educational support for grandchildren, adds a layer of purpose and fulfillment to financial planning.
- **IMPORTANCE IN LEGACY PLANNING**: Aligning finances with family values is essential in ensuring that one's legacy and wealth are passed down in a manner that honors those values, benefiting preferred causes and initiatives.

- **LEADS TO PRUDENT SPENDING**: Investing in areas that reflect family values, such as sustainability, can result in more meaningful and financially wise decisions with long-term benefits to both the environment and personal finances.
- **FINANCIAL SATISFACTION**: There is a deep sense of fulfillment and peace of mind in knowing that financial decisions and allocations are in harmony with the family's core values, enhancing overall financial satisfaction in retirement.

CHAPTER 33

DECIDING WHERE TO LIVE

Choosing where to live in retirement is a decision that extends far beyond finances. Unfortunately, I've witnessed individuals make mistakes when it comes to this critical choice. Allow me to share their experiences. Retiring and hastily relocating elsewhere can prove to be a misstep. As a resident of Virginia, I've noticed many retirees flocking to Florida. These individuals sell off all their possessions in Virginia, uproot their lives, and invest in new homes in the Sunshine State. Yet, all too often, they find themselves longing for their old home, missing the familiar embrace of Virginia. Consequently, they make the expensive and stressful decision to sell everything in Florida and return home. Undoubtedly, this is not the ideal way to begin one's retirement. Let us learn from their experiences and approach our golden years with a more thoughtful and measured perspective.

THE VALUE OF TESTING THE WATERS

A well-considered approach is beneficial while deciding to relocate during retirement. Before making the leap to move to a new part of the country, it's advisable to spend ample time exploring potential destinations. Consider renting a place and staying there for several months to truly soak in the lifestyle, culture, climate, and overall ambiance of the neighborhood. Engage with the local community, frequent the local businesses, and get a feel for the everyday life. This invaluable first-hand experience can provide a clearer picture of what your life could look like in this new locale and help you make an informed decision. Remember, retirement is a significant phase of your life and the place you choose to spend these years should align with your lifestyle preferences, financial situation, and personal values.

GRANDCHILDREN: THE JOY OF PROXIMITY

One of the most joyful experiences I hear retirees frequently speak about is the precious time they spend with their grandchildren. There's an undeniable charm that grandchildren bring to the lives of retirees, a unique blend of youthful energy, innocent curiosity, and pure affection. Being close to their grandchildren allows retirees to witness milestones firsthand, share in their laughter and wonder, and impart their wisdom and life experiences. This proximity not only strengthens the intergenerational bonds but also brings a renewed sense of purpose and vitality to the retirees' lives. The joy of watching a grandchild's first step, hearing their first word, or simply sharing a leisurely afternoon at the park, are the simple yet profound pleasures that make retirement truly enriching. Living far away significantly reduces the frequency of enjoying such experiences.

SUMMARY OF KEY POINTS

1. **RECONSIDERING RELOCATION:** Many retirees move to another state seeking a better retirement life but often find themselves missing the familiarity of their old home, leading to a costly and stressful return.
2. **APPORACH WITH THOUGHTFULNESS:** Relocation in retirement demands a well-considered approach, suggesting the importance of spending time in potential new locales to truly understand their lifestyle, culture, and community before making a permanent move.
3. **VALUE OF FIRSTHAND EXPERIENCES:** Renting in a new area before buying to immerse oneself in the local environment and community is advised to ensure the chosen place aligns with one's lifestyle preferences, financial situation, and personal values.

4. **GRANDCHILDREN AS A SOURCE OF JOY:** Proximity to grandchildren in retirement enhances quality of life by allowing retirees to actively participate in their grandchildren's milestones and experiences, strengthening familial bonds.

5. **IMPLICATIONS BEYOND FINANCES:** Choosing where to live in retirement involves considerations beyond financial aspects—it requires thinking about personal values, lifestyle preferences, and the potential impact of being away from family, particularly grandchildren.

CHAPTER 34

STRATEGIES TO PROTECT YOURSELF FROM FINANCIAL SCAMS IN RETIREMENT

UNDERSTANDING THE THREAT

Often seen as an easy target by scammers, retirees need to be especially vigilant in protecting themselves from financial scams. With the increasing sophistication of scammers, understanding the various types of scams and the tactics used by fraudsters becomes essential. Retirees often fall victim to a range of deceitful tactics, such as fraudulent calls masquerading as law enforcement or phony charitable organizations preying on their generosity. Retirees are often targeted by these deceptive practices, emphasizing the need for vigilance.

RECOGNIZING THE SIGNS OF A SCAM

To stay one step ahead of these scam artists, retirees should familiarize themselves with the key signs of fraudulent activities. Beware of unsolicited contact, aggressive sales tactics, and demands for immediate payment. These are all warning signs that should not be ignored. Regularly monitoring your financial accounts, credit reports, and transaction alerts can quickly help you identify and report suspicious activities. It is of utmost importance to bear in mind that reputable organizations will never require immediate payment or solicit sensitive information through unconventional means. Similarly, they will not request money in the form of gift cards or wire transfers.

BUILDING A TRUSTED NETWORK

Moreover, retirees should build a trusted network of individuals who can provide advice or second opinions on financial decisions. This network may include family members, friends, or professional financial advisors. Before making any significant financial commitments or investments, retirees should consult this network. Additionally, seminars on financial security and fraud prevention can provide them with updated knowledge and strategies to safeguard their hard-earned money. After all, a proactive approach is the best defense in this ongoing battle against financial scams.

SUMMARY OF KEY POINTS

Guarding against financial scams is an essential aspect of retirement. As retirees often have substantial assets and may not be as tech-savvy, they are a popular target for scammers. Here are some strategies to protect yourself:

- **BE WARY OF UNSOLICITED CONTACTS:** Retirees should treat any unsolicited calls, emails, or messages with caution, particularly if they involve aggressive sales tactics, demands for immediate payment, or requests for personal information.
- **REGULAR MONITORING OF FINANCIAL ACTIVITIES:** It is crucial for retirees to keep a close watch on their financial accounts, credit reports, and set up transaction alerts to detect and act upon any unauthorized or suspicious activities promptly.
- **EDUCATE YOURSELF ON THE TYPES OF SCAMS:** Gaining an understanding of the common scams targeting retirees, including those impersonating law enforcement or fake charities, equips you with the knowledge to identify and avoid these traps.
- **CREATE A TRUSTED SUPPORT NETWORK:** Building a network of trusted family members, friends, or advisors can provide retirees with a valuable resource for advice and second opinions before making any financial decisions or commitments.

- **PARTICIPATE IN FINANCIAL SECURITY SEMINARS:** Attending seminars on financial security and fraud prevention can offer retirees current information and strategies to protect their assets and identify scams effectively.

CHAPTER 35

ENSURING A SAFE AND FALL-FREE RETIREMENT

UNDERSTANDING THE RISK BEYOND FINANCES

Throughout this book, I have extensively discussed the topic of financial risk and its direct impact on your money, decision-making, overall well-being, and quality of life. However, it is critical to acknowledge that the most significant threat to quality of life for my clients is not solely rooted in financial risk. As a financial expert, I strive to stay within my area of expertise, but I feel compelled to address a major issue that I have observed retirees facing. They may be leading their lives without any major issues until they experience a fall.

THE REALITY OF FALLS AND THEIR IMPACT

A simple internet search on *Falls for Retirees* will provide you with a wealth of alarming statistics and accompanying resources to learn more about fall prevention. The truth is that falls are not uncommon, and a significant percentage of people will experience them, often resulting in significant consequences. Even individuals in the prime of their retirement years have unexpectedly fallen, leading to surgeries and medical emergencies. These incidents underscore the importance of fall prevention, particularly for retirees and seniors. It is worth noting that falls can also have psychological impacts. The fear of falling can hinder physical fitness, contribute to social isolation, and even lead to depression among retirees.

Age certainly plays a role, but falling is not limited to what we typically consider as seniors. During my early thirties, I had a mishap at my house, specifically with its old-fashioned staircase at the entrance by the front door. While descending the stairs, I slipped and partially tumbled down. Despite my youth, fitness, and overall good health, the incident left me with bruised and potentially fractured ribs. It took a full six weeks for me to make a complete recovery. As a result, I found myself feeling quite apprehensive about traversing stairs for a while. This experience enabled me to empathize with the physical and psychological impact that someone may endure following a significant fall.

CAN FALLS BE PREVENTED?

The truth is, not all falls are avoidable, but some can be. The key lies in dedicating time to education and taking precautionary measures. Fortunately, there are resources available for fall prevention that offer valuable guidance. It is easy to believe that such an incident could never happen to you, especially if you are fit and active. However, the reality is that accidents can occur. I have witnessed people falling during adventurous trips abroad in their first few retirement years, requiring medical attention in foreign countries. Additionally, I have come across numerous cases of individuals falling due to their pets inadvertently tripping them, leading to joint replacements and surgeries.

MITIGATING RISKS THROUGH PREVENTION

As we age, our physical strength and balance may decline, increasing the likelihood of falls and the severity of resulting injuries. Falls can range from minor bruises and fractures to severe head trauma, and they can also have psychological impacts. The fear of falling may cause retirees to limit their activities and social engagements, resulting in decreased physical fitness, social isolation, and the potential onset of depression. Therefore, it is crucial to implement preventive measures to mitigate the risk of fall-related injuries in older adults. These measures may include regular exercise to maintain strength and balance, identifying and removing potential hazards in the home, and scheduling regular health check-ups.

INVESTING IN YOUR FUTURE SAFETY

Investing time rather than money can yield invaluable returns. Take the time to educate yourself on fall prevention, both in your home and in your daily life. This investment could safeguard the happy retirement you have envisioned and worked toward.

Here's a resource that will help you learn more about preventing falls.

- **NATIONAL INSTITUTE ON AGING (NIA)**: The NIA offers a wealth of information on fall prevention, emphasizing the importance of regular exercise, managing medications, and making homes safer for older adults.

SUMMARY OF KEY POINTS

1. **THE UNDERESTIMATED IMPACT OF FALLS**: While the discourse around retirement often revolves around financial readiness, this chapter brings to light the significant and underestimated threat falls pose to retirees. It underscores that falls, whether due to an accidental slip or health-related issues, can have serious consequences, both physically and psychologically, hampering the quality of life and independence in retirement.

2. **PREVENTION AND EDUCATION**: The chapter emphasizes that, though not all falls can be prevented, many can be avoided through education, awareness, and taking precautionary measures. Resources such as the STEADI program offer invaluable guidance on fall prevention, stressing the importance of being proactive in safeguarding oneself against potential falls.

3. **INVESTING IN SAFETY**: Highlighting that investing time in learning about fall prevention can be as crucial as financial planning for retirement, the chapter encourages readers to prioritize their physical safety. By exercising regularly, removing household hazards, and undergoing health check-ups, retirees can significantly reduce the risk of falls, thereby ensuring a safer and more fulfilling retirement period.

CHAPTER 36

PLANNING FOR THE INEVITABLE

PLANNING FOR THE SURVIVING SPOUSE

This section of the book focuses on living your best life during retirement. You may wonder why it also includes a section on planning for your death. Well, I expect that since your someone who values planning, it's important to know that your spouse and family will be taken care of if something happens to you. By including this section, I aim to provide you with the peace of mind that comes from being prepared. It's about ensuring the security and confidence that a reliable plan is in place for the inevitable.

THE IMPORTANCE OF PROACTIVE PLANNING

Responsible individuals are driven by their desire to safeguard the well-being of their loved ones, even in unforeseen circumstances. This admirable quality is a testament to their exceptional character and genuine care for those around them. It's no surprise that many of my clients, who have diligently saved and planned for the future, possess this remarkable trait. So, what steps can be taken to ensure the security and protection of their cherished ones?

SELECTING THE RIGHT TEAM OF ADVISORS

One essential aspect is choosing a team of advisors who share the same perspective. Selecting committed advisors who will be there when needed the most is vital. Instead of opting for advisors nearing retirement who may pass on their business or delegate clients to junior advisors, consider working with professionals who will be there for the long term. Be sure to include your spouse in meetings with your professional team so everyone is acquainted, has a working rapport, and on the same page.

KEY CONSIDERATIONS FOR ENSURING THE WELL-BEING OF A SURVIVING SPOUSE

Recognizing the inevitability of mortality and planning accordingly is essential to safeguard the well-being of one's spouse in their absence. Here are some key considerations:

LIFE INSURANCE

Maintaining active life insurance policies during retirement can provide financial support for the surviving spouse, covering expenses and maintaining their standard of living.

ESTATE PLANNING

Having an up-to-date will or trust that clearly outlines the division of assets and possessions is critical.

HEALTHCARE DIRECTIVE AND POWER OF ATTORNEY

Ensuring there is a legally binding document in place that outlines medical treatment wishes in case of decision-making incapacity is important. Similarly, appointing a power of attorney can allow the spouse to manage financial or legal affairs, providing peace of mind during challenging times.

JOINT OWNERSHIP

Considering joint ownership with rights of survivorship for major assets like homes or bank accounts can simplify the transfer process upon death, bypassing the often lengthy probate process.

PENSIONS PLANS

When choosing between single-life or joint-life payout options for a pension, a joint-life payout typically provides a lower monthly payout but guarantees continued payments for the surviving spouse's lifetime.

KEEPING YOUR SPOUSE INFORMED

Ensuring the spouse is aware of all financial matters and knows where to find important documents and passwords is crucial. Regularly reviewing the financial situation together can help the spouse feel more prepared and confident in handling matters in the event of one's absence.

CONCLUSION

Proactive planning for this challenging time can help alleviate some of the stress and uncertainty that a spouse may face, allowing them to navigate those tough days while being financially confident. Making sure that the necessary documents are in place and the spouse is aware of all financial matters can provide a sense of comfort during difficult times. Ultimately, it's about giving your cherished one peace of mind and security for when you're gone. By taking steps to do so, you'll be providing them with an invaluable gift—a well-thought out plan to guide them through.

SUMMARY OF KEY POINTS

- **PROACTIVE PLANNING**: The chapter emphasizes the importance of proactive planning to safeguard the well-being of loved ones, highlighting the need to prepare for unforeseen circumstances that could impact a spouse's financial security.
- **ADVISOR SELECTION**: It discusses the significance of selecting a reliable and long-term team of advisors, stressing the choice of younger professionals or advisors with established teams to ensure sustained support.
- **FINANCIAL AND LEGAL PREPARATIONS**: Detailed advice is given on maintaining life insurance, creating a well-organized estate through up-to-date wills and possibly trusts, establishing healthcare directives and power of attorney, and considering joint ownership and pension plans that favor the surviving spouse.
- **INCLUSIVE APPROACHES:** The chapter underscores the importance of keeping the spouse informed about financial matters, ensuring they know where to find important documents and passwords, and involving them in regular financial discussions.

CHAPTER 37

HOW RETIREMENT REALLY STARTS—THE TRANSITION TO RETIREMENT

The transition to retirement rarely unfolds according to plan. The actual act of leaving work can be unpredictable and full of surprises. Perhaps you find yourself with a new manager or your company goes through an acquisition, resulting in a culture that doesn't align with your desires, prompting an early departure. Or maybe one Friday afternoon as you return home, you suddenly realize you're done, leading to a retirement on Monday without a backward glance. There's also the possibility of informing your manager about your retirement, only for them to break down in tears and plead for an additional six months, to which you ultimately agree. The key takeaway is that having a plan instills confidence. When opportunities arise, you can make decisions with assurance, fully understanding the implications rather than blindly choosing a path.

FLEXIBILITY IN RETIREMENT PLANNING

Starting to prepare for retirement doesn't mean that everything has to be set in stone. It's important to have a plan, but it's equally critical to stay flexible, as surprises are often part of life's journey. Being flexible means being open to change and prepared to adapt your plans to new circumstances. Ensure your financial strategy has built-in flexibility and that your income sources in retirement can be easily adjusted.

PREPARING FOR THE UNEXPECTED

Remember that the most reliable plan is one that can adapt to changes. Having a contingency plan in place for unexpected events such as health issues or a sudden market downturn can help maintain your financial stability.

BEYOND FINANCES: ENVISIONING RETIREMENT

Finally, don't forget that retirement isn't solely about finances. It's also about what you envision for this next phase of life. Whether it's traveling, starting a small business, or spending time with family, your aspirations may change over time. Be flexible and open to these changes, building them into your retirement planning process. Flexibility ensures that your retirement will be fulfilling no matter how your dreams evolve.

PART-TIME CONSULTANCY

If you hold a high-level managerial position or have significant responsibilities within your company, it's likely that you possess specialized knowledge of considerable value. When you leave the company, they may express interest in retaining your expertise as a consultant and compensating you for your valuable insights. While this arrangement has proven successful for some, it often remains temporary in nature. After all, retirement signifies a desire to step away from work obligations. While it can provide financial rewards for a short period, it's not advisable to rely on it as a stable source of income. Valuable knowledge has a limited lifespan and may lose its significance after just a year or two of absence.

CONSIDERATIONS FOR BECOMING A CONSULTANT

If you're considering a consulting role with your previous employer in retirement, it's important to weigh the pros and cons. On the positive side, consulting can provide additional income, keep you intellectually stimulated, and maintain your professional network. It allows you to utilize your specialized skills while offering the company valuable expertise. However, there are a few essential factors to bear in mind.

Firstly, consider the flexibility of the role. One of the perks of retirement is the freedom to set your own schedule, so ensure you aren't sacrificing this flexibility. A consulting arrangement should ideally allow you to decide how, when, and where you work.

Secondly, remember the need for balance. While consulting can be rewarding, it should not overshadow your retirement lifestyle or keep you from pursuing activities you enjoy. You might find it helpful to limit your consulting hours or to only take on projects that truly interest you.

Lastly, consider the stability of such a setup. Consulting roles often have a time limit and are not guaranteed to last. Hence, it is crucial not to overly rely on the income from these roles to fund your retirement.

Remember, retirement is a time to relax, explore, and enjoy life. If consulting aligns with these goals, it can be a beneficial arrangement. But if not, know that it's okay to walk away and fully embrace your well-earned retirement.

TELLING YOUR COMPANY

As a responsible individual, it is unlikely that you would simply fail to show up on Monday or abruptly quit over the phone. Therefore, allow me to provide you with some guidance on how to inform your company about your intention to retire. Communicating your retirement plans to your employer is a significant milestone that necessitates thoughtful consideration and careful planning. It is crucial to approach this conversation with professionalism and respect. Here are some effective strategies to help you navigate this important discussion:

1. **CREATE A RETIREMENT PLAN:** Prior to announcing your retirement, it is critical to possess a clear vision of your future. This entails comprehending your financial standing, being aware of your retirement dates, and having a solid grasp of your post-retirement pursuits. By doing so, you can bolster your confidence in your decision, knowing that you are acting in your best interest rather than doubting yourself.

2. **TIMING IS CRUCIAL:** Choose the right time to announce your retirement. Avoid times of high stress or major company transitions. Your announcement should come at a time when it can be properly addressed, and its implications considered.

3. **SPEAK TO YOUR MANAGER FIRST:** It's respectful and professional to inform your direct manager about your retirement plans before anyone else in the company. This gives them ample time to plan for your departure and find a suitable replacement.

4. **PREPARE A WRITTEN NOTICE:** After informing them verbally, provide a formal written notice detailing your last working day and expressing gratitude for the opportunities the company has given you.

5. **OFFER YOUR ASSISTANCE DURING THE TRANSITION:** Make it clear that you are willing to assist in the transition. Whether that's training your replacement or documenting your responsibilities, your assistance can help ensure a smooth transition.

6. **BE PREPARED FOR A COUNTER OFFER:** It is common for companies to make counteroffers in order to retain valuable employees. It is important to consider in advance how you would respond to such an offer. I have witnessed situations where people were taken aback and received enticing offers.

Remember, announcing your retirement is not just about informing the company of your departure. It's also an opportunity to leave on good terms, preserving relationships and reinforcing your legacy within the organization.

PART VI

FINDING THE RIGHT FINANCIAL PLANNER

CHAPTER 38

DECIDING WHETHER OR NOT TO GET HELP FROM A PROFESSIONAL PLANNER

Successfully managing your finances in retirement can be achieved either independently or with the assistance of a financial advisor. Think of it as undertaking a major repair on your home—if you possess the necessary tools, skills, and desire, you can likely handle it on your own. However, if you lack these resources, it may be prudent to enlist the help of a professional. For some individuals, attempting to manage their finances alone can lead to disastrous outcomes, while for others, it proves to be a fruitful endeavor. If you should choose to seek out the assistance of a financial professional here are things to look for:

MARKS OF A GOOD FINANCIAL PLANNER

1. **EXPERIENCE IN RETIREMENT PLANNING:** A good financial advisor has extensive experience in retirement income planning and understands the unique financial needs of retirees.

2. **CLIENT-FOCUSED APPROACH:** The advisor prioritizes the client's needs and objectives over any personal gains, ensuring the client's best interests are always at the forefront.

3. **RELIABILITY:** The advisor is dependable and can be relied on for accurate, up-to-date advice and information.

4. **STABILITY:** They provide consistent and steady advice, maintaining a calm and pragmatic approach even during turbulent market times.

5. **TRANSPARENCY:** The advisor is upfront about their fees and discloses any potential conflicts of interest.

6. **STRONG COMMUNICATION SKILLS:** They explain complex financial concepts in simple terms and keep the client informed about any changes in their investment portfolio.

7. **PROFESSIONAL CREDENTIALS:** The advisor holds relevant certifications and stays updated on the latest financial planning trends and regulations.

8. **HOLISTIC FINANCIAL PLANNING:** They consider all aspects of the client's financial situation and provide comprehensive financial planning rather than focusing solely on investments.

CERTIFICATION

If you want to find a good financial advisor, one easy way is to start by finding a **CERTIFIED FINANCIAL PLANNER™**.

Becoming a CFP® professional requires a blend of education, experience, and ethics. First and foremost, prospective candidates must have a bachelor's degree in any field, but they should ideally have taken courses in subjects like finance, economics, or business.

Following their undergraduate education, they must complete a comprehensive course of study at a college or university program registered with the CFP® Board, covering a range of topics from tax planning to retirement and estate planning.

Subsequent to this program, a candidate must accumulate at least 6,000 hours of professional experience related to the financial planning process, or 4,000 hours of apprenticeship experience that meets additional requirements. This experience provides practical, hands-on understanding of the theoretical knowledge gained during their studies.

Additionally, all aspiring CFP® professionals must pass the challenging CFP® exam, which tests their ability to apply financial planning knowledge to real-life situations.

The exam encompasses over 100 topics, including stocks, bonds, insurance, tax planning, and retirement planning.

Lastly, candidates must agree to adhere to the CFP® Board's code of ethics and standards of conduct, which put clients' interests first. They must also disclose any past or pending litigation or arbitration, regulatory investigations, bankruptcies, liens, and other potential conflicts of interest.

Thus, becoming a CFP® professional is a rigorous process that combines formal education, practical experience, and a commitment to ethical standards, ensuring that those who earn this designation are well equipped to provide competent and reliable financial advice.

A CAUTION AGAINST ADVISORS WHO RELY ON THE 4% RULE FOR RETIREMENT INCOME PLANNING

An advisor who exclusively promotes a *Sustainable Withdrawal* strategy for retirement income may demonstrate a lack of understanding of essential elements or a risk level that is higher than what you may be seeking. These overlooked elements include managing *Sequence of Returns Risk*, tailoring plans to meet the client's individual needs, adapting to market fluctuations, and managing risks related to longevity, healthcare expenses, and inflation. This may also indicate a lack of experience in retirement income planning, a crucial trait for effective financial planning. Thus, relying too heavily on a sustainable withdrawal strategy raises concerns about the advisor's knowledge and ability to offer dependable, comprehensive, and secure retirement income planning. It suggests that the advisor may be simply regurgitating the sales pitch from their investment department instead of providing personalized advice based on what is truly best for you. While many advisors follow this approach as the primary option, it highlights a lack of specialization.

A CAUTION AGAINST ADVISORS WHO RELY ON ANNUITIES

An advisor who relies solely on annuities may lack the necessary experience and depth of understanding that you require. While their product may address the risk *of Sequence of Returns*, it fails to consider inflation and other retirement risks we have examined. Annuities are typically offered by insurance companies. Some financial advisors are essentially insurance agents who label themselves as financial advisors. Many of them began their careers by selling life insurance and now offer annuities and perhaps some investments. However, they may lack the skills and capability to provide comprehensive financial planning for your retirement. These are the types who often host sales presentations with free steak dinners, inviting you to learn about a specific product without even knowing your financial needs, other than generic demographic profiling based on your age and address. If you have ever attended a timeshare presentation, you know what to expect from this.

CHAPTER 39

ABOUT THE AUTHOR

ABOUT ME

In the final analysis, my tenure as a financial advisor during turbulent times such as the great recession and the recent COVID-induced downturns has been more than a career—it's been a calling. Specializing in aiding those on the cusp of retirement, I've strived to ensure a seamless transition for my clients to a future rich in potential and financial stability. My tenure, at my firm Hunt Country Wealth Management has not just been about number crunching; it's been a journey of partnership, guiding individuals along the often complex road to a confident retirement.

With a planning strategy built on the core values of reliability, flexibility, and stability, and a clear emphasis on transparency, we've managed to foster a trust that is paramount in the advisor-client relationship. Our team, skilled in retirement income planning, moves beyond the conventional advisory role, providing tailored strategies that adapt to changing market conditions and personal circumstances, ensuring our clients' retirement plans are robust against the uncertainties of longevity, escalating healthcare costs, and the specter of inflation.

Reflecting on this journey, it is clear that success in financial planning is not merely about adhering to a single investment philosophy but rather about adopting a holistic approach, one that considers a diverse array of options to meet individual needs. At Hunt Country Wealth Management, we pride ourselves on being listeners first, advisors second—committed to offering dependable, personalized advice that navigates our clients toward a financially confident retirement. It is my hope that through these pages, you've gained insights into not just my professional ethos but also the profound sense of responsibility I feel towards each individual who seeks my guidance. In the realm of retirement income planning, navigating potential financial pitfalls with acumen and care is not just a service—it's a promise.

TAKE THE NEXT STEP

If you're poised at the brink of retirement or aiming to solidify your financial future, we invite you to reach out. Embark on a path where fear of the unknown transforms into confidence in what lies ahead. At Hunt Country Wealth Management, our commitment is to you—your dreams, your security, your legacy. Schedule your consultation today to discover how our tailored strategies can illuminate your path to a confident retirement. Together, we can build a future not just survived, but thrived.

Exclusive Resources and Educational Materials

At my firm, Hunt Country Wealth Management, our mission is to empower individuals with the knowledge to make informed financial decisions. I am thrilled to extend these additional complimentary resources and educational materials to my readers.

Explore these two exclusive tools to enrich your financial journey:

Discover essential strategies and steps for planning retirement with our **FREE Retirement Guidebook™**. Access it at huntcountryinvestments.com/retirementguidebook/ and find our the most important shift you need to make to your finances when you retire.

Enroll in our comprehensive, no-cost course, **Retirement Basecamp™**, at huntcountryinvestments.com/retirementbasecamp/. This course offers a detailed guide through the intricacies of retirement planning and will help you establish a roadmap.

I encourage you to take advantage of these resources. I hope they provide you with additional insights and help you forge a path toward a secure and well-planned retirement.

Here's to your successful journey!

CHRIS MERCHANT BIO

Chris Merchant, CFP® BFA® MBA, is the founder of Hunt Country Wealth Management and a seasoned veteran in the financial services industry with over two decades of experience. With an MBA in finance and economics, Chris is a **CERTIFIED FINANCIAL PLANNER™** professional and Behavioral Financial Advisor™, as well as the bestselling author of *On Investing Well: The Elements of Good Investing*. He is distinguished for his experience in a sophisticated income planning approach known as time-segmentation. His broad client base extends to a diverse range of individuals including leaders in Fortune 500 companies, entrepreneurs, pilots, nurses, and educators, all of whom benefit from his personalized approach to retirement planning. Chris's mission is to transform retirement journeys into experiences of clarity and direction, to help ensure a secure and enjoyable future for his clients.

804 Amherst Street Winchester, VA 22601

https://huntcountryinvestments.com

DISCLOSURE PAGE

Securities and advisory services offered through Commonwealth Financial Network®, Member FINRA/SIPC, a Registered Investment Adviser. Fixed insurance products and services are separate from and not offered through Commonwealth Financial Network.

The opinions and forecasts expressed are those of the author and may not actually come to pass. This information is subject to change at any time, based on market and other conditions and should not be construed as a recommendation of any specific security or investment plan. Past performance does not guarantee future results.

Diversification seeks to reduce the volatility of a portfolio by investing in a variety of asset classes. Diversification does not guarantee a profit or protection from losses in a declining market.

Asset allocation does not guarantee a profit or protection from losses in a declining market.

This book contains hypothetical examples which are provided for illustrative purposes only and do not reflect the performance of an actual investment.

All guarantees referenced are based on the claims paying ability of the issuing company.

Annuities are long-term, tax-deferred investment vehicles designed for retirement purposes. Guarantees are based on the claims-paying ability of the issuer. Withdrawals made prior to age 59½ are subject to a 10 percent IRS penalty tax, and surrender charges may apply. Gains from tax-deferred investments are taxable as ordinary income upon withdrawal. The investment returns and principal value of the available subaccount portfolios will fluctuate, so the value of an investor's unit, when redeemed, may be worth more or less than the original value. Optional features available may involve additional fees.

Exchange-traded funds (ETFs) are subject to market volatility, including the risks of their underlying investments. They are not individually redeemable from the fund and are bought and sold at the current market price, which may be above or below their net asset value.

Investments in target-date funds are subject to the risks of their underlying holdings. The year in the fund name refers to the approximate year (the target date) when an investor in the fund would retire and leave the workforce. The fund will gradually shift its emphasis from more aggressive investments to more conservative investments based on its respective target date. The performance of an investment in a target-date fund is not guaranteed at any time, including on or after the target date.

Investments are subject to risk, including the loss of principal. Environmental, social, and governance (ESG) criteria is based on a set of nonfinancial principles in addition to financial principles used to evaluate potential investments. The incorporation of nonfinancial principles (i.e., ESG) can factor heavily into the security selection process. The investment's ESG focus may limit investment options available to the investor. Past performance is no guarantee of future results.

The fees, expenses, and features of 529 plans can vary from state to state. 529 plans involve investment risk, including the possible loss of funds. There is no guarantee that an education-funding goal will be met. In order to be federally tax free, earnings must be used to pay for qualified education expenses. The earnings portion of a nonqualified withdrawal will be subject to ordinary income tax at the recipient's marginal rate and subject to a 10 percent penalty. By investing in a plan outside your state of residence, you may lose any state tax benefits. 529 plans are subject to enrollment, maintenance, and administration/management fees and expenses.

This material is intended strictly for educational purposes and is not a recommendation for or against cryptocurrency.

Made in the USA
Monee, IL
04 November 2026

67381835R00138